RUGBY & ART

RUGBY & ART

Jean-Pierre Rives

Richard Escot

Translated by Robert Pralle

SPORTS
BOOKS

Published by SportsBooks Ltd
August 2015

SportsBooks Limited
9 St Aubyns Place
York
YO24 1EQ
United Kingdom
Tel: 01904 613475
e-mail   randall@sportsbooks.ltd.uk
Website   www.sportsbooks.ltd.uk

Cover designed by Alan Hunns

A CIP catalogue record for this book is available from
the British Library.

ISBN 9781907524493

Print and production managed by Jellyfish Solutions.

INTRODUCTION

One of Jean-Pierre Rives' favourite writers, the novelist and sports journalist Antoine Blondin, regretted that sporting champions, very much a phenomenon of the modern world, should be looked upon as simple heroes, without ever being treated as personalities, like the literary characters one has become used to since the time of Balzac and Hugo. It seems that writers would rather steer well clear of having to 'grasp the enthusiastic beginnings from which an athletic career springs'. But no sportsman, or rugby player to be precise, is necessarily bound to a single field. He can speak straight to the heart, the head, to gut instincts. He can experience the pulse of life without having to hold a ball in his hands. This is the caste to which Jean-Pierre Rives belongs; gifted with emotion, he is capable of feeling, arousing and sharing it.

In 1983, as part of the Avoriaz "fantastique" film festival, Lars von Trier was presenting his sepia opus – Element of Crime *– as outside a snowstorm swept the mountains. The slides had been put away, the skiers were frozen stiff and the pistes had vanished from view. Jean-Pierre Rives was due to take part in a radio broadcast and the presenter, who was well informed, had asked me to go along with his guest, to ensure that he was reminded of the time the live transmission was to be broadcast from a studio temporarily set up at the resort. This was* *how, feeling a little timid at the prospect, I first made the acquaintance of this distinctive personality, unhurried but subtle, gifted with an idiosyncratic quick-wittedness, and at once both staggeringly straightforward and formidably complex.*

I had not noticed before how he leans to his right. It was as though he might tumble over at any moment. Nevertheless, he pressed on, drawing energy from this imbalance. The possibility of an imminent fall was strengthened by the gusting wind. It was shoulder to shoulder that we forced our way across the open space. Visibility was not good, and it billowed white and was cold. I can no longer remember the reason for exchanging the comfort of a heated room for an inhospitable outdoors. One could see the swirling snow getting whipped about with increasing intensity. This reduced visibility did not appear to encourage a postprandial saunter. But, moved with an overwhelming desire, and perhaps feeling a bit claustrophobic, Jean-Pierre Rives wanted to go out. Quite possibly he had decided that the conversation with the passing acquaintance in which he was engaged had reached its conclusion and was not worth pursuing. Nothing, it seemed, was going to change his mind. Certainly not the storm. As it mounted, so did his determination, which was characteristically undemonstrative, but final.

As we made our way across this passage of snow he did not so much confront as get down into the groove of it. A few times a particularly violent blast of wind would deflect our faltering, cold and white, night march, but

Jean-Pierre did not lose the thread of his anecdotes and, in spite of the wind's whistles and roars, would continue with a series of shaggy dog stories which passed from elephants on the loose in the English countryside to a bust of Stalin made of pure platinum. 'The kind of stories,' he says, 'that would not be much appreciated at a soirée, but which are the funniest of all.' And so we arrived in a little bar with frozen noses, our wool hats as rigid as wood and our eyebrows like stalactites. We ordered two coffees. In the restaurant section rock singer Bernard Lavilliers and his team were finishing their meal and we joined them to share some of the warmth around the fireplace.

~

Jean-Pierre Rives will not speak about rugby; about himself even less. Sidestepping these subjects, he leaves the impression of someone shedding a load. One almost ends up wondering if there was in fact a time when he did play. If, occasionally, a witness claims they saw him running around a pitch in shorts, he has a way of convincing them this is just a trick of their imagination. In spite of which, the mystifying Mr Rives was once a prince of rugby. Everyone can remember his blond panache, his explosiveness with the ball in his hands, and his ability to transform base lead into gold in the moment that he intervened, with innate understanding and anticipation, in the action. Realising that verbal communication is to rugby what oil is to painting, he did not limit his own just to the field: the talks he gave

3

utilised simple words, which he would bend about and weld together in unusual combinations, to good effect.

At the dinner that followed the 1984 Five Nations encounter with Ireland, in which a key moment had been the sending off of Jean-Pierre Garuet, the Lourdes prop, for what the referee considered to be foul play, the president of the French Rugby Federation, Albert Ferrasse, described the wrongdoer as an 'imbecile'. When his turn came to speak to the gathering, Jean-Pierre Rives, then captain of the French side, responded that, in his opinion, 'Jean-Pierre Garuet was a loyal player', to whom he dedicated this victory. This produced a round of applause whose significance was not lost on the usually maladroit President Ferrasse; sensibly he did not return to the charge. He knew that if their verbal combat was fought to the point of surrender, then Jean-Pierre Rives, a past master in dialectic, would have him spitting out his words ...

The priceless player – and blond like himself – Jean Salut, upon whom Jean-Pierre modelled himself when he was getting going, did not hide his admiration – 'There was no one like him for creating a winning position out of nothing' – to a journalist on the trail of the young Rives, the winger with something lyrical about him, as if he pictured the game as a great cavalcade: windswept hair, broad-chested, head up, with a swerve of the hips to baffle the opposition defence ... In the course of his career he had caught up with and then overtaken his heroes, Jean Salut, the Toulouse wing forward and French international from 1966 to '69, and Jo Maso, the great centre and fly-half, *later the French coach for sixteen years. Inevitably, Rives would plunge headfirst into the sulphurous regions, then emerge from the seething volcano of the pack, his head covered in blood, his shoulder battered. It was as though he had an overpowering need to explore the earth beyond others' limits, before retiring in peace, to never speak of what he had once seen.*

~

There are three books devoted to Jean-Pierre Rives, biographies published shortly after his career ended. These draw mostly on the testimony of others – his friends, family, teammates and opponents. The subject, whether as an amnesiac who remembered little of the sport, or, with modesty, gliding over the details of his private life, always had much less to say. Neither disclosures nor any stirring of the pot disturbed the myth. Typically perhaps, he had come to rugby at the prompting of his father, who hoped that 'it would wake him up,' at an age when most players have already sketched out the beginning of a career. The impression he conveys is of being a plaything of circumstance, bobbing around like a coconut out at sea. He lets on about originally playing in some scrappy games and not understanding the rules properly. Everything happened by chance he seems to suggest: the best means of discovery.

As an adolescent he qualified for the French Junior Championship at Roland Garros. Although he got to the final, more pleasure was to be taken, aged thirteen, from taking the metro on his own for an educative stroll along the Grands Boulevards. Seeing a neon sign advertising a festival of magic he stepped inside Olympia, Paris's famous music hall. Back in Toulouse it was the conservatoire that his mother, sensing his musical talent, had him enter. And then his father took him along to the rugby. Sluggish though he may have seemed at that time, Jean-Pierre overcame his reservations and, rather than being the anticipated failure, the experience provided a completely new path for him to follow. The story has shades of Jules Renard's Carrot Top *who, lost and alone, steps out in the middle of the night. He intends letting the chickens out of the coop, but, instead, hears that, from now on, he is going to have the responsibility of shutting them in every evening.*

Jean-Pierre has been involved in his share of matches de poules *[French Championship games]. On Sunday he would be there to round up his opponents and, snuffing out their offensive intentions, shut the door in their faces. Diving in head first, his shirt invariably covered in mud, his only ambition was to be invited back the following Sunday. No problem there. His parents, who were living in Africa, knew nothing of his growing reputation, helped along by glowing newspaper articles which complimented him upon his natural talents as a flanker. This rise, which he achieved by himself without any further encouragement or indeed any praise, also had something in common with Carrot Top's story, in which the boy's father, Mr Lepic, criticises the*

6

composition of letters home that he finds too liberal in their use of the upper case; that have no date and whose lines are all uneven but which, worst of all, seem to mock the very convention of sending a regular letter. But all the time, the boy was writing to him in verse.

~

'It is ultimately no bad thing that children should occasionally be misunderstood by their parents! The opposition it entails teaches them irreverence, without which intelligence cannot develop,' wrote Alain-Fournier, author of Le Grand Meaulnes, *at the beginning of the last century to Jacques Rivière, editor of the literary review* NRF (La Nouvelle Revue Française). *In passing, two devotees of rugby. Adulated without limit and heaped with praise for qualities he did not recognise himself as possessing; loved by people, men and women alike, who, quite often, didn't have the first idea about rugby, he was also hated for being different, a quality he cultivated with finesse. Hated, too, by those who could never match his allure and charisma or the virtues of courage, of heart and soul which he represented. With an artist's gift he was able to craft a personality which, although elusive and impossible to categorise, was never less than appealing. All of this goes to explain why he walked away – never to return – from the narrow bounds by which sportsmen are constrained. It did not seem to count that the course of his ten-year career as a French international was lit by victories that were like so many stars.*

His exploits speak for themselves. From the debut at Twickenham in 1975 to his last encounter, facing the Scots at Murrayfield in 1984, Jean-Pierre Rives played fifty-nine times for France and left a similar mark on the Five Nations to Jean Prat, ten years a French international and nicknamed 'Mister Rugby', before him. The resemblance between 'Casque d'Or' – literally 'Gold Helmet' – and the nickname given to Jean-Pierre Rives by the late journalist Roger Couderc, and 'Mister Rugby' went beyond their shared physical attributes and intermediate size that made both of them, as part-forwards, part-backs, ideal for linking play between the two lines. There existed first of all a common approach marked by giving one's all, the drive to play to the highest standard and by sacrifice – not forgetting the notion of the group, which both set great store by. From having captained the Tricolores *for thirty-four games, one can gauge the aura of this out-of-the-ordinary flanker, his intensity and the example he was capable of giving. By his attitude or with a word or gesture he instilled confidence and conquered doubt.*

During his first match at the Parc des Princes the crowd started chanting his name. Not so surprising when one considers that with four inch-perfect passes, three jarring tackles and two sallies through the opposition's ranks he had shown certain key facets of his game. His debut in 1975 just overlapped the retirement of the previous generation, forever associated with an undeniable romanticism. This was the epoch of Jo Maso, Jean Trillo, Jean-Louis Bérot and Walter Spanghero, who had raised the idea of a specifically French way of playing or 'French Flair', for which we were rightly envied by the Anglo-Saxons, to a new level. Following the briefest of intermissions, coach Jacques Fouroux's new generation formed: a pack as hard as nails, consisting of Gérard Cholley, Alain Paco, Robert Paparemborde, Michel Palmié, Jean-François Imbernon, Jean-Claude Skrela, Jean-Pierre Bastiat and, last but not least, Jean-Pierre Rives, digging down into himself to come up with what a Spartan style of play demanded. In an earlier, flamboyant period, the Toulousain had not deprived himself of the space offered by attack. Now he was transformed into a dutiful frontline soldier drawn dauntlessly to wherever the battle was at its most intense. As a ruck or a maul formed, he would be right inside it. A place not a few players preferred to avoid. His stamina was put at the non-stop service of his teammates and his presence, never far off the ball, was by itself enough to transform an unpromising situation into its opposite.

In 1977, using just fifteen players from the beginning to the end of the tournament, France achieved her second Grand Slam. The XV formed an exclusive club with an unbreakable bond of friendship, as the onward march of an hermetic style of play inspired both respect and fear in their opponents. If the French public witheld its affection and proper appreciation from the team, any criticism left Jean-Pierre Rives unfazed. Even then he possessed a natural ability once a game was over and he had showered and changed to no longer be interested by it.

~

Forgetfulness, in his case, is a virtue. It is a method of getting rid of surplus to retain the essential, of what takes itself to be serious, to retain what actually is, and of the useless to keep a hold of what matters. Three pm, not before, is when his clock chimes. Then, as if by magic, when the final whistle brings it to an end, the game has vanished. No need for post-mortems to draw the match out. That was no doubt how he was able to keep reproducing performances whose intensity was so admired and then to quit the scene and to make a life for himself outside rugby.

In 1970 France's schools side had been hit by a wave of injuries that sidelined most of its third row. So Jean-Claude Joubert, the trainer at the time, was obliged to call on one or two regional hopefuls who had yet to be selected. A director of the Committee for Midi-Pyrénées recommended that he should contact this blond kid with excess vim. If the boy was smaller than average, he compensated for this by being in perpetual, overflowing motion and with crushing tackles. Joubert listened to the advice and soon after noted the arrival of an unusual-looking fellow wearing a wool hat pulled down over his ears. It was hard to tell whether he was half-asleep or in a kind of trance caused by the cold. Following two training sessions in which he had not especially shone, he was given a place on the substitutes' bench in the lee of the wind. Destiny may have been at play when, after just a quarter of an hour, one of the starting line-up had to come off injured and the coach, not without reservations, had no choice but to call on this unusual 'little' gentleman, cocooned in his lethargy, to go and warm up. The seventeen-year-old Jean-Pierre Rives shook himself down, lifted off his wool hat and, with cursory swinging of arms, ran onto the pitch. 'To my astonishment, he was the best of those thirty players,' recalls the coach. 'Then when the match was over he went back into his shell and didn't say another word. As if he had not played in the game. As if he was elsewhere.'

'Elsewhere'. No other word fits quite as neatly. Capable of agreeing to a third meeting because he has forgotten the previous two planned for a single appointed hour, Jean-Pierre Rives does not like to say 'No'. Nevertheless he has a full complement of wariness. His massive inertia serves as camouflage against bores. He is as sparing with words as he is profligate in giving his time. His humour is deadpan but he will also offer succour to the stray dogs which he encourages to come and sit by his woodburner. Sculpture has given him a means to keep on creating and to remodel the world he sees around him. The work may take an hour, a day or a week.

~

Not all are allowed to approach Rives. His world and way of life have been constructed with a degree of artistry. Without imposing himself he will put out feelers; cast his line to see if the other will follow it or not. It is a way

*of recognising kindred spirits. 'I cannot stand silence,'
he acknowledges. Only when others are around does he
fully come alive. To join this circle it is first necessary
to understand certain unwritten rules he has made:
his regles de 'je'. Constant demands are made on his
time and he is no stranger to admirers who will not let
yesterday go, even as he fights to live in the present and
to leave the 'celebrity' player he once was in the past
where he belongs. Still they keep coming to bask in his
reflected glory, hoping that some of his stardust will rub
off on them. Because Rives' most natural characteristic
is his generosity, he does not refuse them the light.*

*Impossible to pigeonhole, and often difficult to track
down or get hold of on the telephone, Jean-Pierre Rives
will always leave a scent for his friends to pick up.
These old companions often move along with him and
do not seem to have any trouble sorting out rendezvous,
whatever the delays and improvisations involved. Bibi,
Denis, José, Pierre, Jeannot, Gaston, Thierry and one
or two others. With the exception of Patou, gone to join
the great scrum in the sky, this inner group of friends is
most likely to be found at the artist's workshop, known as
the hip hangout, which moved from Châtillon via Gare
du Nord, to end up in Sèvres. It is well hidden away,
though there is nothing deliberate about that: the door is
always wide open.*

*If you share his enthusiasm for an art that intertwines
lengths of curved steel, he will lead you out into his
yard to have a look amidst the irregular piles of rusting
joists, that under his regard will come to life. According*

to the way they bend together, he picks out the shapes he considers best and which, in his head, he is already arranging, fixing and welding. To understand Rives one should remember that time for him is not a succession of defined moments, neatly joined together. Maintaining a distance at nearly the same time that he takes a plunge, he is fully engaged with the present – as well as being a nostalgic. There is not just one Jean-Pierre Rives; certainly not the one people expect; that would be too simple. As in a novel, his way would not have been the way it is commonly understood to be nor, equally, unknown as it is to the majority of people, without an element of mystery, plenty of surprises, a dash of insouciance and, occasionally, the highest aspiration. Jean-Pierre Rives plays host to a nature of which he is not always in charge and of deep emotions that are always capable of coming to the surface when he is least expecting them to ...

His silences and wary sighs, designed to mark off an area that is to remain private, hint at abundant non-subjects and deleted memories. Here, he seems to be (silently) saying, begins my existence, my intimate world. Which is why he has only ever talked about what everyone knows already. Given that he had not yet definitively rejected nor accepted the proposal of a book based on a series of conversations, I continued to canvass the idea to him. 'Drop by the atelier. We will see ...' That is when I discovered that the Rives of silences hides another who is at ease with and playful with words. It gratifies him to murmur them. And that is the way he not so much speaks to as confides in one, *punctuating his sentences with an occasional flourish. It is as though he fears that, were he to raise his voice, then he would snap an invisible thread which, alone, is carrying him along. Reading back the interview transcripts all his responses appear finely chiselled, like aphorisms. Where it may look as if some editing has taken place, in fact his original words were weighed with precision. His, occasionally puzzling, sentences bear the personal mark. French President Léon Blum once wrote of Jules Renard that 'He has a unique style, which no one can mistake. No author has turned over familiar conceptions with such a light foot.' 'Everyone should have a copy of his Diary on their bedside table. As well as the novels of Antoine Blondin. He has written seven. Not prolific, but he has touched on everything that matters,' assures Rives.*

~

There exists an unlikely relation between Rives and Renard. Take the apparent contradictions of the battler turned artist, idiosyncratic but friendly who, in spite of being impervious to pain, can be stung by criticism. He had to change his natural attacking game to become an uncompromising defender; was a dreamy pupil before turning into a captain – still introverted but able to galvanise his team. Doesn't all this exemplify the force of Jules Renard's belief that 'If you wish to be sure of always doing your duty, undertake the tasks you find disagreeable'?

At Auckland against New Zealand in the famous match of 14 July 1979 honour was at stake, not to mention pride and the desire to get back on even terms, following a lame performance in the first encounter. Nothing could have stood in the way of Captain Rives leading the main training session like a fanatic; completely out of character for someone with a natural aversion to this kind of group session. He ran out in front in a controlled rage, his face a mask, driving the team behind him to the point of exhaustion. Two days later the French side achieved its first ever victory in a test in New Zealand. In pushing himself beyond his normal limits, Jean-Pierre Rives won over the team, who would now follow him wherever he led. Normally he would not command anyone to do anything. Away from the field he had always declined from imposing his opinions or his way of living. But he was set to be captain of France for six seasons.

Before, his determination had been directed at keeping the ball alive. Now he was at the service of others too. In the 1980 Pretoria Test he was wounded against the Springboks. He returned to the front still bleeding steadily, like a poilu, *or French soldier in the First World War, through a bandage wrapped around his head. It was to become a famous image. Compensating for a relatively ordinary physique when compared to southern hemisphere mammoths he had an élan, a taste for the extreme which could border on recklessness; it left his teammates with no choice, when he went to pound hard at a defensive wall much higher than himself, than to head into the hot zone themselves – either to follow his example or to save him, as the situation required.*

The bloodstained warrior with a puffed-up face also knew, when freshly shaven and wearing a dinner jacket, how to convey a fashionable image for this tough guy's sport practised by gentlemen. Trilingual, cultured and with a ready wit at his disposal, he cut an elegant figure about town in Paris, rubbing shoulders with the world of showbiz as if nothing could be more natural. Thanks in part to these encounters that took him beyond sport's limitations, it is not so bizarre that he suddenly became interested in art.

~

In rugby, a contact sport, it is not easy to maintain an unchanged side. The exceptions, such as the French XV of 1977, are rare. More typically the group splits apart and a fresh team is brought together in improvised fashion. Whatever their differences, the players must try to settle them as best they can. The altruistic and easygoing Jean-Pierre Rives was second to none in getting diverse elements working together. Four years after the Grand Slam was secured by a unit of fifteen, he won a second Five Nations with a disparate team that mixed young and old, quiet and effusive. It is hard to think of anyone else orchestrating that achievement. He was able to count upon his friend Robert Paparemborde, a soul mate who could not have been more different in terms of build, character and background. So in 1981, this unlikely phalanx managed to bring off a spectacular success, just as the sans-culottes once had at Valmy [the battle in which the revolutionary army gained its first victory in 1792], hoisting tolerance higher within the ranks of a French team than it had ever stood before.

As a child Jean-Pierre fainted rather than raise the subject of a peritonitis-induced pain in his stomach. Later, he once more pretended to feel nothing when his shoulder was fractured. Though he had grown up now, nothing had changed. He was not about to make a fuss if it came to a few gashes or a dislocated shoulder. The heart of the matter was that he vehemently refused to be the cause of play being held up. Knocked out, covered in blood – but still upright – he would never accept leaving the pitch. One day in South Africa, to the referee wanting him to regain his senses and leave the field, he responded: 'And go where?'

Down in Australia he played the second test of the 1981 tour against the Wallabies with a broken shoulder. His arm hung loose and his pale colour was the accompaniment to a martyr's agony: he could not imagine abandoning the teammates who were both his comrades and (sporting) family. The example he thought it his duty to show went as far as the calvary. Not that he harboured illusions of this Christ-like dimension, which, in spite of himself, he nevertheless seemed to share. In the ongoing adventure first begun in Toulouse he was determined to go to the very end; if the price for remaining in the company of sporting men was to wear a crown of thorns he was prepared *to pay it. On the other side of this coin – represented by his willingness to undergo physical torments on account of a faith in maintaining this sporting connection – for example being trampled upon by a stampede of red-shirted gnu – he would never accept that a single person should come and sully the high ideal he held of the sport.*

Ill-intentioned opponents would seek out his face with their boots, and, unobserved, slap him hard. It was not unusual for some within the sport's hierarchy, since they could not pinpoint any weaknesses, to find fault instead in his qualities, or a perceived cheek, aggravated by playboy looks. Each of us has an opposite for whom our qualities are viewed in an entirely different light. Where we savour, the other itches with impatience; he inevitably dislikes what pleases us, is jealous where our passions are concerned, actively hoping that they burn out; he belittles our aspirations and casts a negative spell on them; sometimes he goes so far as to damn us. Some, of course, are more fortunate than others and do not cross paths with this opposite. Unluckily for him, Jean-Pierre Rives often came up against jealous and bitter individuals.

Amongst them was an official manning the turnstiles during the 2002 Six Nations. Standing on his authority, he would not allow Rives into the Stade de France to watch the England game, under the pretext that presenting an invitation to the previous encounter was not the same as a valid ticket. Hard to imagine such a scenario. The most likely explanation was that he had given his ticket to a friend whose need was greater, without thinking he was doing anything particularly wrong. 'The kiosk was blue, the ticket red and the collector dayglo yellow. He made me think of an oversized firefly lit up in neon, with hair coming from all directions: out of his ears ... eyebrows as thick as his moustache. The match was due to kick off at any moment, which left just him and me. Otherwise the stadium had breathed in everything around it. The ground itself trembled as the random crowd noises rose to a din. Perhaps a try? Then for whom? It was like love in the dark; fireworks with the sun high above; sound but no picture. And the whole time the collector was studying the ticket, whose date did not match the day. I was in the process of not watching a game which had taken place a month before. If only I had arrived earlier and he had been in position later ...', he wrote, letting off steam at the expense of punctilious officials for the benefit of the monthly Le Monde de Rugby's *readers. For someone with such a defective memory, Jean-Pierre Rives still knows how to harbour a grudge. It is a further paradox but he generally keeps a check on this tendency, by pardoning in others what he will not tolerate in himself. This indulgence partly explains the goodwill and empathy that continue to come his way. On this occasion, however, the man who had given so much to the game was obliged to head home. Instead of seeing the match, he had stood in line like everyone else. Neither liberty nor utopia, his two talismans, had prevailed at the turnstile. In this kind of situation, where he is opposed, blocked or hemmed in, rather than becoming worked up, Jean-Pierre Rives often prefers to respond with his ready wit. He concluded his description of this particular one with the deadpan observation:* 'à guichet fermé' – *'sold out' – could equally mean, 'Let's not talk business'.*

~

Amongst those challenged when it comes to enjoying the good life and who, by their very attitude, present the same challenge to others, only one got him jumping up and down: a Welshman named Winston Jones. Perversely chosen to referee a decisive encounter between France and Scotland for the 1984 Grand Slam, it was the first time that this puny-looking man, lacking in natural authority, had officiated an international. It was also thanks to Mr Jones, who found the task beyond him, that the French captain was deprived of an historic third Grand Slam to add to those of 1977 and 1981, which would have raised him just a little higher in the pantheon of French rugby.

Deprived is no exaggeration. Fifteen years after the game, John Rutherford, fly-half and later coach of Scotland, confided to me that he and his teammates were consistently and deliberately offside, so as to nip France's attacking surges in the bud. In other words, they had the wit to profit from the referee's inexperience and turn the French over. Rather than provide closure for Jean-Pierre, the belated confidence not only justified but reignited his heated feelings vis-à-vis this wretched authority figure.

Having begun his adventure in the national side with a free bird's insouciance, Jean-Pierre Rives was more like an inflamed rooster when he took off the team shirt, with its emblematic coq, *for the final time. He headed off without a backwards glance and left the next generation to its joys and sufferings.*

Not only had he left his decade-long mark in the most celebrated grounds of the world – Auckland's Eden Park, the Loftus Versfeld in Pretoria, Twickenham and Parc des Princes – but he also did unstinting service keeping the precious ball in motion on some less well-tended pitches, whose barren surfaces turned his knees and elbows raw: those of Toulouse Olympique Étudiants Club, Beaumont-de-Lomagne, Stade Toulousain – where, in partnership with Walter Spanghero and his friend Jean-Claude Skrela, he produced the most dashing back row witnessed in French rugby; then, finally, the Racing Club de France, whose glory days he was central to reinstating.

One never gets more generously served than by oneself: so, wishing to start a club devoted to the true spirit and enjoyment of the game and which aimed to play an expansive and attacking game and maintain their old camaraderie, he and his 1977 Grand Slam mates founded the French Barbarians, a team with neither address, pitch nor clubhouse. The plan was to be open house to those who both wished and deserved to join in, and to put on a triple blue hooped shirt – France, Oxford and Cambridge – unadorned by sponsors' logos. The French Barbarians were now better placed to maintain this spirit than their British counterparts who, during the professional era, had seen marketing make inroads into their original ideal.

The guiding light of this fraternity – which, around the '77 core, brings together players who had once been, at least superficially, at odds, like Jo Maso and Guy Basquet, in the company of others as diverse as André Boniface, Serge Blanco, Denis Charvet, Fernand Cazenave, Marcel Martin, Daniel Dubroca, Laurent Pardo, Éric Champ and Serge Kampf – is Jean-Pierre Rives. At the age of fifty he can still surprise. If he considers his Barbarians ideal to be in good shape, he will suddenly vanish from the face of this oval-shaped world, to go and discover a challenging golf course or to gaze down from a Balearic Isle onto the blue Mediterranean, flat like a sheet of glass. He has been known to act – if you look closely enough there he is beside Christopher Lambert in Vercingétorix, *as the chief of a Germanic tribe. And every now and again he gets the urge to write, for example, 'on an aeroplane, where I will scribble things down on the paper sick bags provided'. As in life, so in art: he sculpts after his own, unbiddable, fashion.*

~

It does not take long reading these interviews to notice that Rugby & Art *is a spontaneous piece of work. Most of what you read here is a first take, with just the occasional overdub added on. A few notes are provided for readers less well acquainted with rugby history. He never tried to pretend that a book can be produced just by* talking, however entertaining and well expressed one's words might be, and then putting the written version between covers. He enjoys literature too much to dress these conversations up as anything other than the frank exchange that was ours over a few weeks.

It was not clear at the outset if there was much to be gained talking, once more, of rugby, at a time when he is still attempting to put an end to the perception people continue, nearly thirty years on, to hold of him as a sportsman. The desire to finally cordon off the oval ball with its uncontrollable bounces was certainly a factor in talking, which at least allowed Jean-Pierre to work through his feelings, which were not altogether straightforward. So we came to have our first rendezvous at his workshop in the rue Pajol, which he was in the process of moving from, and to continue at his new address in Sèvres, to talk, when the moment seemed right, of one or two things he knew about rugby. For the record, our rapport was not automatic at the outset. Instead there were long periods of silence, in which I was implicitly led to understand what the rules of the game were to be. I also began to understand, as the welding sparks flew in my direction and I unavoidably became smeared in loose rust and grew exhausted holding the metal members as he looked for their points of equilibrium – what could be described as my apprenticeship – that Jean-Pierre has other tools at his disposal than those one necessarily sees.

'Has it gone too high?' When there is a lull in our rugby talk, he takes another look at the steel pieces, *charting their climb that stops just short of the fifty-foot-high ceiling; pieces that owe their character to their tight winding relation and seem to join the earth and the sky, out to the horizon and up into the clouds. They are like keys to who knows what doors, which is no doubt what makes them so mysterious and attractive. They might even say more about him than he, talking at length, does ... Both are best appreciated by observing the spaces lying between the lines and sentences.*

Unlike the majority of sportsmen, both before and since, he has succeeded in living his life the way he wants to. This book bears his mark. With a great deal of reserve and a dash of English humour, the correct amount of hidden meaning and not a few allusions, he leads the conversation in the direction he would like it to go; which does not mean he leaves his demons unattended. There are many who consider him superficial. It is he though who proposes that we should follow him down to certain depths, from which one does not always return unscathed. The schoolyard where he was picked upon, for example. He talks about what truly irritates him but contrives, in a unique fashion, to pull off melancholy with a smile. If it is him indicating the direction to follow, his instructions remain imprecise, since he would rather wander off down byways and along parallel paths. What could be better than rugby as a joyful, vital way of building your own community and of discovering your own tribe?

'I have nothing more to say ...' That was not altogether true. With the twin exception of the first and the last, he omitted to talk about the fifty-nine internationals

he played in. What he does talk about is the friendship, the tolerance, the right to reject conformity and to be different, encapsulated within those two limits. The trace he leaves is more that of a golden halo than of statistics and records.

'So, have I gone too high?'

Richard Escot

I was not cut out to play rugby, which was what I ended up doing for fifteen years.

If it was not for being blond, then I would not be who I am.

And if I hadn't been who I am then maybe I would not have played rugby.

Therefore, the likely reason that I am a rugby player is that I am blond.

Jean-Pierre Rives

1

A Sunday with a perfect blue sky. In front of the workshop entrance, chicken pieces sizzled slowly on the barbecue. To its side stood a spread of fresh salads, raisins and a rich chocolate cake, a square of thick cardboard serving as a tablecloth. The meal over, we headed back into the vast space, that had previously been a factory, to prepare some coffee. Jean-Pierre Rives, cup in hand, was finally prepared to talk. It had taken several days during the course of the previous few weeks for us to obtain the right mood, that is to say unanimity. Each time I visited he had carried on matching and welding the rusty lengths of steel he works with, suggesting I should come back the next day. There was always work for me! Until now – the moment at which he decided he would talk about himself. So we settled down face-to-face on this cloudless day, my apprenticeship finally served.

~

Jean-Pierre Rives, how would you describe rugby?

Above all, it's a matter of attitude. Almost a way of life. With a very strong sense of sharing that is symbolised, amongst other things, by the pass. I don't think that it's at all possible in such a game to be happy in seclusion. The alchemy at work is more developed than you might think. In this sport you are declining the verb 'to be' in fifteen, twenty, maybe even more different ways, not just 'me' and 'him' ... That's the way in which I would describe rugby. The way I see it, the sharing is the most important part. I am talking of the active not the passive voice. Each player has to respect and be respected for what he is. The right to be different is an important one. Sharing then complements it. That's what rugby is about, not organising a uniform group that would most likely be mind-bendingly tedious. So while the game is about sharing, at the same time I think one is casting a look around oneself. Rugby is engaging with others.

You emphasise the importance of sharing. In what way is that value more typical of rugby than any other sport?

I emphasise it because it is through sharing that men – and not only rugby players – get to the essence of life. Sharing is at the heart of things and rugby helps to bring out what we have in common rather than what divides us into our little camps. That's what sets it apart from politics, in particular, and life in general: the possibility of realising something together.

What exactly?

Bringing people, who otherwise might have little in common, with different ways of looking at life, together. Rugby provides a common bond for them. And if that's all the sport achieves, then it's already done something. For me, at least, that is the essential. What can be better in life than to provide a basis of unity for those who are otherwise divided by so much?

How does rugby achieve that better than other sports?

Sport generally succeeds in bringing people closer together who have different points of view. How does rugby manage to do it a little more? The answer is the intimacy of combat ...

Were you conscious of rugby's values straightaway, or was it only after you had played enough games and by personal maturing that you grew to appreciate them?

I don't think I had an immediate appreciation of what rugby was all about. To be honest, not even the first idea. Without knowing why, I was naturally drawn to it. And then I discovered something which, though I was not yet fully committed, appealed to me.

What was that appeal?

Everyone has an activity which interests them,

in which they can become passionately involved. Looking back now, I can see that rugby was the one thing capable of carrying me beyond my limitations. I saw myself in a new light. Becoming passionately involved in sport revealed a part of me I had not been conscious of beforehand.

What did you discover?

That my happiness was no different from others'; that my problems were no different from theirs. They don't guarantee success but without this common appreciation and fusion a team is not going to achieve much. Those looking in from the outside should not judge the group motive too harshly. There comes a point at which one needs to identify with a family, social group or ideal. Being part of a team provides that. And when everything taken together runs smoothly one can achieve some extraordinary moments, a state of grace almost. It happens occasionally. Not all the time, of course. Sometimes never. But when that fulfilling moment arrives, rugby players, whilst not actually gods – there is no need to exaggerate – are at least in their company.

When you first played, what surprised you the most?

I had the feeling that time came to a standstill. Both as it passes by slowly and as, over time, it accumulates. In a way, people are separated by time: there are the young and there are the old. But when playing rugby, all those differences seem to fade away. Oddly enough, this sport permits adults to remain children, and children to grow up faster.

What were you like as a child, before you started playing rugby?

You would have to ask my mother ... As far as I can remember, I was rather inhibited and solitary. Not always very communicative. That hasn't changed a lot (*smiles*). Maybe I was on the shy side. A lot of the time I am still reserved.

Jean Dauger says the beauty of the game is how it forces a man to find himself ... Was that your case – that, thanks to rugby, you managed to push yourself forward?

I don't know if I ever forced anything. It seemed to happen of its own accord. Naturally. I was amazed to find that no age difference, or even generation gap, was able to separate men who at some point had been rugby players. As though they all belonged together. You know, while rugby may not be universal for all, there are those for whom it is universal. For an hour and a half on the pitch, as well as before and after, we are all thinking in a similar way. Some are lucky enough to be playing rugby at the moment, others aren't, because one cannot play forever. But something still remains.

What exactly?

A number of years ago, when I was still playing, I think I once said that the game was hardly complicated. Either one kicks the ball between two posts or one runs with it and touches down behind a line. Today, now that I have forgotten everything I used to know about the game, I would say that rugby is basically to do with a ball surrounded by a few men. Once there is no longer a ball, what remains is the men.

So what lies at the heart of rugby is the desire to be with others, to be immersed with, in fusion with them and to no longer feel that one is alone?

Yes, and that is something very important, which goes beyond the playing field. It couldn't be more topical. More than ever we need to respect this essence and maintain certain principles, even if rugby has turned professional and needs the money. We need to carry on appreciating what is most noble in the sport and maintain its basic principles, without which there can be no rugby. Instead there is the risk we will end up with something different and, however good that is, it will not, as far as I'm concerned, be the same game. It is unlikely I would recognise myself in it.

If rugby was to lose its values you would no longer be interested in it at all?

Don't get me wrong. I am not here to give lessons. I am simply taking stock of what I see. There are still plenty of good things happening, I know. Memorable moments are still conjured up. I have seen some fantastic team play, stars in my eyes. If there's a young boy or girl somewhere in the world who is able to live their dream a little, then it's definitely worth continuing making the effort.

As a teenager you were inspired by the kind of player Jean Salut was, a wing forward and blond like yourself. Is it important to have a model you can look up to?

I was inspired by quite a lot of players; by Jean Salut, but also by Jo Maso. Others too ... But I was most inspired by the game itself. I would like to have been involved in it, to have shared some of the quality those players had.

Who would you like to have been?

Jo Maso. I wouldn't have minded being Jo Maso at all. But I never had that kind of talent, nor his qualities.

But you yourself are a model! Now the youngsters want to be Jean-Pierre Rives. For them you are very significant ...

They think I am, but that's something completely different. Jo Maso was an outstanding player. People may think that I was an outstanding player. But it is not true. I would like to have been Jo Maso. I wouldn't have minded being Gareth Edwards, either. I was simply lucky enough to play with men whom I admired. To be on the same field – by whatever miracle – and what is more, to become a friend of theirs. That's quite a story, you know!

You want people to believe that you do not consider yourself their equal?

I am not lying to you. I am not interested in creating a legend of myself. I am telling you the truth. That is all.

The fact remains that of all the former or current rugby players you are the best known, the most recognisable. The most celebrated, in a word.

People don't remember anything. They have heard it said ... They think that being Jean-Pierre Rives is fabulous. But, being in the best position to tell, I can say to you: I have my doubts whether it is really as great as all that. How real is the memory people have of me? I was never the personality that they seem to remember me as. I know deep down that I was never that person, but they carry on taking me according to this idea they have. Something way beyond who I really am. I wouldn't mind being the Jean-Pierre Rives that they imagine me to be myself ...

But in the eyes of everyone else, and in spite of your modesty, you are that Jean-Pierre Rives.

My modesty ... my modesty ... I am not so very modest. (*He flares up*) If I had been that strong, I would have known, wouldn't I? Do you hear me? (*Becoming grouchy*) And that's not what we're here to talk about ...

Jean-Pierre, I think that, on the contrary, it's a very interesting question ...

(*Emphatically*) Well, I don't think so! And I do not want to discuss it; I already have to live with it ... (*He becomes reasonable again*) For a long time people would ask me what colour my Rolls-Royce was ... Obviously they imagined that I was rich and famous. When that first started I would reply that I didn't have a Rolls-Royce, but I could tell that no one was listening. However much I insisted that I was not rich, I was not believed. So that they would leave me in peace, I had to offer some reply. From then on, I started to say it was this, that or the other colour. The thing was that if I inisisted that I did not have a Rolls, not only would they remain convinced that I was rich, they would also think that I was a liar (*smiles*) ...

Yet, however you feel about it, you are one of a handful of French sporting legends.

That is a fact I have to live with. I must reconcile myself to having this extravagant reputation as a symbol of rugby and to being touched as though I could heal the sick. You might not believe this, but I have occasionally heard people when encountering me, talking amongst themselves, saying, 'Come on, we must go and touch him.' I know only too well that I am not that man. The way they see me is far beyond my real character.

You say you would like to have been Jo Maso. Why particularly?

For his nature and for the openings he was capable of conjuring. The centre game is rugby played in the way that I like it. I would love to have played at centre, in the three-quarters, but I was not good enough. When I asked my coach, Jacky Rougé, whether I could, he replied to me, 'OK, but only five minutes, while the others have the ball.' Because he knew that I was just a tackler. I didn't think that was very nice (*smiles*) ...

What do you like about centre?

Everything! The attitude, elegance ... They are the really gifted players, capable of doing anything. And intelligent.

You respect their panache?

Absolutely. Their attraction is their panache. I would rather be the attacker, the centre finding openings and creating chances, than the workhorse always running after, trying to catch them. So when your trainer says to you, 'Play in the centre but stick to tackling,' imagine my disappointment, my feeling of inadequacy ... After that, the only role is a supporting one. You do the best you can. (*Silence*) There ... That's my story.

You described the pass as a symbol of sharing. Would you agree that it is the centres who are the most generous of all and who have raised the skill almost to an art form?

A good pass is one that reaches its destination. But if one adds to that the style with which it is delivered, then we probably are talking about art. That is where the French are privileged and lucky enough to play a particular kind of game – their game. You only have to mention certain names: André Boniface, Jo Maso, Jean Trillo, Philippe Sella, Denis Charvet ... It's not a coincidence if those at the centre of the game are also at the top of it.

But – and here we go again – you also hold a place amongst that host of great players ...

My story's not the same as theirs. Not even in the

same ballpark. Thanks to one or two ideas that matter to me I was able to rival men much stronger than me. Maybe it would take a psychiatrist – or perhaps even a pair of them – to try and understand that. There's something which I feel I lack. And at some point that feeling, allied to my sensitivity, is going to express itself. One way or another. If such a want can't find an elegant outlet or emerge as real talent, then too bad – it is going to be expressed all the same. I need to do my thing too ... I bend my lengths of steel and I weld them together. The result can weigh a lot and may not be especially aesthetic. But it's there and it needs to be produced, because I don't have any intention of stopping. It is as the result of will that anything happens. And where there's a will, there's a way. It's not always about being elegant. It can be a struggle, too. It can be either.

Is your need to express yourself simply a matter of sensitivity?

There is something inside me that needs to be expressed, but I think that's the same for everybody. Who doesn't experience that desire, that lack of self-sufficiency? When you connect it with a certain sensitivity, then you have something that needs to come out into the open to be real. All of us have that inside, something special that needs to be expressed.

Rugby first allowed you to express yourself. Did you have the feeling that this sport was going to play a big role in your life and that it would help bring something inside you to light?

Not exactly, no. Because what I did on the pitch was separate from the rest of my life ... It still is. I can run on two completely different voltages. When I do something I do it without running through all the consequences. And that seems to work.

How did you first become involved in rugby?

I owe a lot to Jacky Rougé. Above all, he gave me the desire to come back for more. My father had taken me along one Sunday, saying, 'This will wake you up!' They handed me a team jersey that more or less fitted. I got on the pitch; I was buzzing all over it, not letting up on the opposition for a moment. So Jacky Rougé said to me: 'You must come back on Thursday!' Which is what I did. In an instant I felt that I had interested someone. If, on the other hand, he had said to me that Sunday: 'Listen lad, this isn't really the game for you,' I would not have played rugby again.

When did the sport's epic nature, the sense that it was an Odyssey-like story, with its heroes and myths, first dawn on you?

Later, much later ... I was slow in appreciating the mythology because I had not been brought up within the tradition of the sport. I had no idea about it. The day I was selected for France 'B' I was not even interested in going to the team talk. I preferred to spend some time with my friends, because I wasn't aware of the significance of that meeting. I had not yet latched onto what it meant.

Was there a moment when it struck you that you were in fact a rugby player?

Somebody said to me: 'You realise that you are a top-level sportsman?' Personally, I thought of myself as a Sunday player. Nothing more. I thought about playing the game and that was all. Whether it was a Sunday game – or a Saturday game – or the big event that an international is did not mean that much to me. What I am trying to say is that the game came to me in a natural way. Nowadays, top sportsmen have an intensive training schedule. All I did was to make sure I played sport every day. Not necessarily rugby, but some sporting activity. That is the way I had been brought up: one played sport.

In some ways you were ahead of your time ...

I am not so sure that what I have done is that important. The reason I decided to talk about my experience is that, ultimately, it is what I am most knowledgeable about. There are other subjects which nowadays interest me more. The reason for recalling all this history with you is to share it with those just getting going in the game. Two or three things that they might find useful. Maybe I can help them save a bit of time ... Apart from that, I have no lessons to give. No message to pass on. I would just like them to know that the dream is achievable. You see, if I have been able to make this great thing happen and to become the friend of people I admire, then anyone can.

2

A glacial wind sweeps around the quays of the Seine. Down by the river, on its Sèvres–Saint-Cloud section, the workshop appears abandoned. A row of rusty-toned sculptures is lined up against the wall. Stacks of rail-shaped beams await unpacking, being separated and then carried inside. That morning the building was open at both ends, inviting the cold wind to swirl in. Looking frozen, Jean-Pierre gets an industrial-sized heater going. Its flame gives off light as well as heat and he takes up a position beneath it, with his knees pulled up to defend himself against the biting cold. He holds a steaming coffee in the cradle of his hands and helps himself to a selection of chocolate patisseries. We resume the interview where he left off the previous evening – because there is no chance of welding in this cold weather.

~

According to you, it is the men themselves, rather than what they do with the ball, who come first. What do they do to become a team? How do they communicate amongst themselves?

A type of identification takes place. The men acknowledge to one another that they all want

44

to come together, to form a group. For all sorts of reasons and sometimes no reason at all. Historically speaking, the impulse to unite around an idea is something that can be either beautiful or dangerous, depending on whether the notion is a good or a sick one. Then the consequences can be terrible. I imagine there are even mechanisms for producing that type of unity ... So a lot of care needs to be taken in this kind of adventure. Fortunately, in sport the situation is unlikely to get out of hand.

In the principal teams you played for – and played a part in – how was this bond formed?

It was fairly straightforward. We would call each other regularly, to talk about organising some fresh idiocy together. We're still at it – which probably makes us a bit dumb, no? At the time, there was a stubborness in the way that we thought of ourselves as a group, the way we stuck by our feelings and, following on from that, our ideas too. Every now and then, we would meet up again. We still do. Usually in the same old place, with the same old stories getting told. It's actually very reassuring (*smiles*).

Is there a particular way in which a team spirit is formed, which you can recognise as it happens?

No, there is no recipe. If there were, we would

be manufacturing, bottling and stacking it on supermarket shelves. There is no magic about it, just one or two basic ingredients. Even with them you cannot be assured that the mayonnaise is going to take. But without oil and egg yolk there would be a bit of a problem.

What are the oil and yolk of a team?

(*Silence*) Maybe one would call that love ... (*embarrassed*) It's very difficult to say, you know. To put it into so many words ... sharing, tolerance, commitment ... I don't know, I am not sure how you would describe it ... Maybe ... (*long silence*) Caring for the others.

A pulse?

I don't know if it's that controlled. More like an epidemic. I think that man is essentially good. He may be capable of making every mistake in the book but, on the other hand, he can behave nobly. And I would say to you that caring for the others is like an epidemic. All it takes is one to start it and everybody ends up happy. We tend to follow a lead, after all.

Where are the emotions you are talking about located: the mind, the heart, in the stomach, on your skin?

It is within you! Completely within you (*as though speaking to himself*). Internal and silent ...

It is reserved ... We're talking about men after all: it's not something that gets discussed. I have never spoken about it. Hardly ever.

Hardly ever, that's a start at least ...

Talking rubbish for the most part.

What kind of rubbish?

Laughable, mostly. Still, the connection has taken place. One knows it is there. Yup. On one or two occasions we experienced it and joined the privileged ones. After that, one is never quite the same again. You feel less shabby than you otherwise would. Indestructible even. It is a great honour. Something of that sort. 'Indestructible' might not be exactly the right word. You have the feeling that you are able to die in advance of others, without it mattering, now that you have placed your finger on something quite unusual. It's very hard to put into words. In an exchanged glance we can tell that we will not be the same again. We have reached the top of the mountain and placed a finger on something soft, that is not hot or cold but is very good. I probably couldn't reach the top of that mountain any more, but I can recognise the man who just has. Words would be superfluous. We look at one another and know that we have both seen the same thing.

Looking down from above?

No: from below, in spite of being up there. You know, one should be careful about looking down from the top too much. People end up seeming very small.

You use lengths when you sculpt. One could say that you have made a business of them, considering that rugby is a game of lines. You have never really changed your line ...

That aspect was always beyond me. I could never participate in the game of lines. I let it pass me by. I always liked it but I was only good at retrieving the ball and resuscitating the game. It's the same with the art I produce. I work with bent and rusty steel left out for days, weeks or months, in all weathers. There are similarities. I want to carry on and so I bend my metal into different shapes and weld the lengths together. That's the path that I'm following and which keeps me occupied. Since I can no longer express myself playing, I use steel instead.

It's not just the three-quarter line. There's the line-out, the front and back row that also make rugby a game of lines. Watching from the stands do you have the same appreciation of rugby as when you were playing it?

I'm not very interested in the aesthetic aspect

of the game. It's the human dimension I am interested in. The one-metre circumference with the ball at its centre is what attracts me. The eyes, glances and facial expressions within that space. The rest of the game, whether or not it's aesthetic, doesn't hold the same appeal for me. No doubt because I could never aspire to it ...

To coin a phrase, you are a rugby myopic.

Yes, but a happy one, who likes the essence that is given off in a ground, the emotions. Apart from that I don't give a damn. The noise of a stadium is enough for me. Afterwards my imagination can do the rest.

When you were a player, were the exchanged looks and everything you could hear around you already part of the enjoyment of the game?

I lacked what it takes to be involved in everything the game had to offer. I was working on the engine, rather than the bodywork and finish. With the engine running smoothly, you can be confident that things will go OK. What line was taken around a bend was not my business. My head was buried beneath the bonnet; someone else had to hold the steering wheel. I was not a very good driver anyway. There were plenty who were better than I ever was. The machine is what interested me and the rest could take care of itself.

It is sometimes said that forwards are down in the hold. Is that a place of suffering, down there by the engines?

I wouldn't say it was a question of suffering. Pain neither. One ought really to be talking about pleasure. Of course there are occupational hazards and it's not always easy. One shouldn't forget: rugby is a contact sport. But let's not exaggerate. When one has been handed an opportunity and a privilege of this kind, it is like one has entered heaven; even if you occasionally receive a smack in the face. When you consider all the Ordinary Joes watching you and the kids for whom you are a hero, it is wiser not to talk about hard work or sacrifice. There is no sacrifice involved there, just pure pleasure. That is the way I have always felt.

Because you enjoyed the game's physical side?

No! No! I trained in order to be ready for these collisions, that's all. I went and worked up a sweat by myself. I was happy to do that. There was no suffering. Not at all.

You gave the impression of being a dilettante, when in fact you kept to a busy schedule to stay in shape. That must have been an effort.

I never found it an effort. The reason for training was that I was involved in a physical sport. It seemed obvious. All I did was to train a bit harder than the others ...

But you never let on about it.

I didn't let on about it because nobody ever asked. No one was following me when I went running ... But nor did I go off surreptitiously. I just happened to be on my own. Having said that, I am a bit of a loner and not that keen on obligations to the regiment.

You are like those writers never seen writing or an artist not encountered in his studio. If I may say, a combination of reserve, not wishing to display yourself, and of pride, wanting to perform in public at the top of your game.

I don't want to be hypocritical. I do have my disciplined workhorse side. When I decide to do something, I do it seriously. After which I go onto the next thing. I can listen to the same piece of music forty-five times, or keep sculpting in my workshop non-stop or serve in the restaurant every night for a month. My excessive side. I focus on something and stick with it. And twenty years ago I used to train twice a day.

Without ever talking about it ...

I think it would have been rather pretentious of me to make a show out of what I was doing. Then everyone would have been asking: why aren't the others doing the same as him? People can think what they like. I simply tried to perform to the best of my ability. Once I had got myself in shape, there was always the question of the match. And when it came to that I was not particularly gifted. My knowledge of the game was relatively limited. Even today, I can feel lost. All I could do was to work away and perform to the limit of what I was capable of. It's the same thing now working as a sculptor or restaurateur: I try to inform myself and then I do the best I can.

What is it about extremes that you find attractive? You seem to take a positive pleasure in them ...

Because I know the way I am.

You enjoy taking things to the extreme?

Not just for the sake of it. With me there is something paradoxical. Let's put it like this: if you were to say: 'Be excessive,' I would probably do nothing. But if you were to tell me that I was rather lazy, then I would get stuck in ...

So, in a word, you are contrary?

That's a bit too Basque, which I am not ... All the same I am more than capable of doing some quite unusual things.

Although you don't like to talk about yourself you have revealed that you were fairly solitary. How was that possible when you were amongst so many people?

I am a solitary who enjoys city life. A loner who would rather not be alone. You can try explaining that if you like! One has to deal with the way one is. I am a reliable soldier who does not like being given orders. I try not to be too serious about it, even when I take on a big project. If I say something I try to anticipate how my words will be taken. I don't want to be taken at cross purposes. I would like what I am actually saying, rather than what I might be supposed to say, to be heard. And then I lay off what I have been doing and confront myself once more and try to accept the way I am. Sometimes it is not easy.

Did rugby help you a lot?

Yes, because it provided me with a way to meet some exceptional characters, who all had amazing, natural, intelligence. Intelligence from the heart: that's what provides the key. The rest is not so important. Everyone has a private side, his thoughts and feelings, his own way of looking at the world. A specific way of saying the same thing, and yet another way of writing it. It's up to each one of us to crack the code. Rugby is a game of excess played by excessive characters: there is no point in hoping for reasonable dialogue amongst such people. If one of the lads gives you a rough slap on the cheek to let you know he likes you, then you give him a boot in the backside to tell him you feel exactly the same. In this sport everyone talks. And they talk loudly. That's what made me realise that we were probably all deaf. Our sentiments tend to be overblown. I have to say it's something which, deep down, pleases me about rugby players who, for all their faults, are fundamentally generous. In word and deed. Even in their sudden impulses; everything. They are very alive. They exist.

So one returns to this attitude, that is close to your heart ...

Exactly. Everything that we have been talking about goes back to the pass, the desire to hand on. That's what I've been thinking about today. Look at the 2007 World Cup: right now its sole interest is that it represents an opportunity to pass something on, to communicate, give and share. The thing to do is to go and find a few kids in Africa, in places like Senegal, Morocco and Madagascar and give them the seats normally reserved for pampered camp followers, who have no pressing need to be there. To show these children some rugby. No: to avoid misunderstanding – I don't really mean that people with tickets should be led away from the stands but, rather, they should at least let these kids sit on their knee or share their seat (*laughs*) ... I was given an unbelievable opportunity. If I can hand something on myself and create a little bit of happiness, I will be pleased. I seriously think that if each of us could make, say, five or six others happy, the world would be a better place. At least there would be fewer problems ...

Do you have the feeling that this sport helped make you who you are and you now want to give something back?

Since I don't have much technical ability, I am not the one to be giving coaching lessons. I don't believe there is a great deal to be learnt by them. Plus, I am a case apart. I was not properly schooled, as various people have reminded me from time to time. Not always in a friendly way. But I can understand that, too.

The example you give is what matters?

It's with what is inside you that you appreciate the essence of the game. Something natural that cannot easily be taught. On the other hand, you can learn a bit of attitude. It may be secondary but its instruction can nevertheless be emphatic. There's a lot you can do with the right attitude. I know one or two men who are great rugby players, even if they have never put on a pair of shorts in their life. I have also run across one or two who did play a little, but without ever becoming rugby players. There is no need to name names ... Rugby deals with them in its own way. It always has and it always will. That kind don't last long in the game!

It is an attitude that has been helped along, as much as anything else, by writers creating tableaux that have helped to generate the myths and develop the history of the game?

Rugby is a part of life and it attracts some of the most gifted authors. I am thinking of the two Denises, Lalanne and Tillinac, Kléber Haedens, Antoine Blondin and one or two others. All remarkable writers. Then there are the Irish: Samuel Beckett and James Joyce, who played a little and knew about the game. I would not claim that if they had never played they would not have become writers, but I like to think they wouldn't have written in quite the same way. We found ourselves in a fairly extraordinary situation as players so our lives became extraordinary. That's what needs to be understood. When one has the luck, the honour and the privilege to live – maybe I should say participate in – these remarkable encounters one has no choice other than to live them in an extraordinary manner. I hold it against certain players that they play the game rather as if they were working for the Gas Board. And let's not forget the *troisième mi-temps* (or post-match craic). It's not just a time to get drunk. It's a time with a special aura, that deserves to be appreciated. Nothing is more important in our game than its version of the nineteenth hole and these moments of grace need to be made the most of. They are not only about getting drunk and setting the place ablaze, trashing restaurants. I know what I am talking about, having attended my share of *troisième mi-temps*, without actually drinking.

To hear you speak it feels like a particular art of living is being described ...

If one wishes to be different, one has to adopt a different manner of living; otherwise, why bother? What you are is simply the way you live. Much better to be than to have. It does not matter what you are doing – playing sport, sharing a moment, joining in a party, or simply participating in life itself – the great thing is that it becomes possible to feel as though time has come to a standstill. Maybe it has. Then when it starts up again, you are aware of just how quickly it moves. That's the reason why those of us who have been privileged are obliged to live the best we can; to be alert to each second.

Not only for ourselves, but for all those who would like to be in our situation but are not. It's as though they can live through us. That's why we do not have the right to disappoint them. These are straightforward people: nothing more, nothing less. There was a poet who put it well when he said, 'Whatever has been promised to children, one is bound to deliver.'

Who are your favourite writers?

I read a lot of Alexandre Vialatte, who I think is fantastic. Once I start one of his books, I can't put them down. And then I reread them. What I like about him is the easy touch he has for dramatic scenes, combined with the truthfulness he gives to lighter moments. I enjoy that continual paradox. The way he uses contrast and opposition to create equilibrium or, viewed another way, an intriguing imbalance. Life and death; light and dense. There are one or two other writers who provide the same pleasure, such as Paul Léautaud or Jules Renard. Everyone should have a copy of Renard's Diary on their bedside table. The novels Antoine Blondin wrote are very good. He produced seven – not exactly prolific, but they cover a lot of ground in a lively manner. I like things which are short but which, using limited means, say a lot. That is what I'm aiming for with my sculpture. The less cluttered it is, the less bad it becomes. I am not operating at the same level as them of course. Nor do I know them personally although, often, I have the impression when reading them that I do. As if I have joined them on the path they are walking along. And, before I forget, David Ferrero deserves a special place as far as I'm concerned. He's got an original way of expressing things. Even more than his writing, I love the way he talks, his manner of spinning a yarn. I am surprised that rugby has not given him a bigger role, that he doesn't appear more frequently on TV, now that Roger Couderc has gone. I enjoy his exaggerations and the tangents he goes off on.

Do you like aphorisms?

I don't like them – I love them. I even come up with the occasional one. But then later I forget them. Fortunately for me they have been recorded by certain friends.

What writing method do you have?

I generally write the same way I eat chocolate: in short, sharp bursts. Scribbling in an aeroplane on the back of sick bags is not unusual. The problem is, as well as an idea, you require paper and something to write with. It's not always easy to combine the three. Writing resembles rugby less than golf, where you can't get started without your clubs and balls, a tee and a glove. One needs to be in the right spot, ready to type as soon as inspiration strikes and later start editing. I don't have that kind of stamina. I am better suited to sketches and reportage, both of which are quick. The elaborate setting up of a premise, drawing it out, then making sure everything fits together is not for me. If I read something somewhere I might get an idea that transforms it and turns the original into my own little creation. Curious, I know. Rather like my sculptures. I begin with a scrap which later goes off in a new direction. Usually it leads somewhere different. There's a rather amusing thought process at play whenever I make a piece. My métier is simply to turn things over.

3

Positioned in front of the workshop entrance, an impressive-looking crane loads three of the artist's sculptures onto a low-loader bound for Béziers. Three monumental pieces that are airy nests of steel. Once the lorry has headed off towards the exhibition at the far end of the country, Jean-Pierre gets down to the day's work. He sweeps the studio's concrete floor in preparation for a new piece. As he is doing so, a young poetess arrives and hands him a bound collection of verses she has written for him in gold ink, illustrated with black and white photos. A stray dog wanders in and makes a circuit of the studio. This appears to make Jean-Pierre happy. A typical moment, whether mundane or special, to which Jean-Pierre will react with empathy before calmly detaching himself once again. He is in a more forthcoming mood than usual. The time is ripe for one or two confidences and to talk about subjects that are close to his heart. First up is the French Barbarians, this club without a home whose members, amongst whom he figures prominently, gather once or twice a season from all over, in the generous spirit which they all share towards the game.

~

At the mention of the French Barbarians' name, it seems that something stirs in you ...

In the beginning was this idea, that has since been discussed a great deal. A bunch of men who, in the past, have all played a bit of rugby and so participated in a real human adventure which they don't, if there is any alternative, want to let go of, decide, in the image of the original, British, Barbarians, to found a club – without a clubhouse maybe, but with the intention that some guys possessing a bit of soul, and whatever their age, race or religion might happen to be, should continue to play. The original idea was a nice one and the story has turned out well. The essential thing about the Babas is that it represents a particular attitude, a way of living. As for the rest, who really cares?

Do you see it as an oasis within a sporting world in which everything is now calculated, and motivated by profit?

It might be an oasis or it could be unrealistic, but there is no question that this dying breed needs good taking care of. What professionalism has achieved is to overturn the way rugby is run, at the same time as affecting its basic principles. I look at the Babas as the guardians of a certain ethic, a certain way of doing things.

One gets the feeling you are worried this rather unusual club might disappear.

No, I am not that concerned even if, as I have just said, the way that rugby is organised has changed. The sport itself still produces the same emotions. It can still make one starry-eyed. Having once played with the fathers and knowing the sons a little now I feel confident in saying that. There was too much good in them to have spawned monsters. I feel lucky to be involved with their offspring, who are fantastic lads. The dads need reassuring and the sons assuring that rugby has not changed. The spirit is there, as it always will be. It's what the sport is about.

Has it been hard keeping the French Barbarians going?

We're giving it everything we've got ... There is a group of us, all committed to keeping this ideal alive in the most practical way we can think of. Professionalising the sport has led to a very crowded calendar. At least that's what people say. Personally I don't feel that it's fuller than it was before. The only difference is that everybody is talking about the game more than before ... The clubs want various guarantees and the players certain assurances. That can make things a bit complicated. We prefer to play *à l'ancienne* – one day a year. It's encouraging to know that the

Barbarians RC exists to inspire both the young and the not so young – meaning some of the best players in the world.

What does playing à l'ancienne *represent for you?*

It's definitely not meant pejoratively. *Au contraire.* It is an attitude to life. We all meet up together; there's no training, we slip on the jersey and go out and play. Look, when you have top players, which has always been the case with the Barbarians, there is not much point in training. I am not sure there's anyone with a great deal to teach these guys. That they need to jump, push and run about a bit? That's not exactly original. If you aren't already doing all those things playing rugby, there isn't much point going out onto the pitch. Plus, training would only tire the players unnecessarily (*smiles*).

It must be fun to get your own team together.

Look, it's them, not me, who make all the phone calls. The Babas is a team conceived by the players for the players. After all, it is they who make a team. The way we operate is by proposing names we have heard about from people whose judgement we trust.

You mean it's a player's co-operative ...

You could say that, yes. They are the selectors

and they tend to select themselves. Flair is the key. These men have enough experience to tell that some players, who you might have thought suitable, would not actually fit. They have certain standards. Baba – that's a self-awarded medal. If one of them feels he no longer merits it, he will probably hand it back. That's the way I see it anyway.

What is your role then?

Neither selector nor committee member, as we don't have either in the normal sense. I am one of a group of guys who, when they get together, take things the way they come. That's all that is required. The players are big boys now, capable of taking care of themselves: there's nothing they need to be taught nor made aware of. They don't have to have things demonstrated to them. They are there because they want to be, to take part and to testify. That's the rugby I am talking about, whose attitude and code can influence other parts of one's life too. We have the right and the responsibility to hand them down; the right to dream and the responsibility to let others dream. The Barbarians are not a bad version of the rugby dream.

Aren't clubs sometimes reluctant to loan out their best players for matches, whose sole raison d'être *is pleasure, where they could, all the same, pick up injuries?*

No, it's stupid to talk about reticence or resistance these days. It's not the central question. Think about this: who is not in favour of the kind of philosophy, the individual style and the code I have just been talking about? The only thing is that everything has speeded up, with the league and cup schedules becoming busier. The clubs have financial considerations and the players may be seen as an investment. Profit plays a big part. But let's not forget the essential, which is that spirit points the way. Money matters and investment considerations do not necessarily have to influence the spirit the sport is played in.

When you meet up with your friends in this special world that you have created and you are confident that you are about to enjoy a fulfilling afternoon, does a change come over you?

Yes, I genuinely feel that those who have had contact with it are transformed in some small way. I think what one leaves behind physically is compensated by the good it does the soul.

And that's how it is every time you play?

These days I am more of a spectator. A cheerful

spectator who can watch the players realising the better emotions, being happy, being fulfilled. Cultivating their patch of paradise. That makes me feel good, having this aim in common. As for the rest, I am not sure, you know, if it really matters that much.

During your playing days, was a part of you spectating even then? Were you able to detach yourself? Or were you so immersed that you had no such perspective on your game?

I can remember part of me observing at the same time I was playing. Even as I was fully involved in the game I was contemplating it. And occasionally I caught myself doing this: playing and watching at the same time. I was never actually looking at myself play but I could sense the split between my involvement in the game and my perception of it. Players have a different perspective to spectators.

What do you still recall about the matches in which you played?

The sensations I experienced then have definitely faded with time and it is the detached element of those contests which I can remember. I no longer have a very good memory of what I did; on the other hand, I can remember the lads I played with perfectly.

Jean-Pierre Rives

You remember watching your mates?

Yes: I saw them. Very clearly. Today that strikes me as being fairly extraordinary. But I cannot summon up any memory of watching myself. As I saw them, I felt lucky to be amongst such company. Jean-Claude Skrela, Jo Maso, Walter and Claude Spanghero, Roland Bertranne, Denis Charvet, Serge Blanco ... for starters. I had the feeling of being this child who had been given the privilege of playing alongside men who were exceptional, not just in the way they played, but the way they were. I was very lucky. I can't say it often enough. I also have no idea what I had done to deserve such an opportunity. I realise that may be hard for other people to accept, but it is genuinely the way I feel.

At the risk of insisting, it seems to me that you nevertheless rank with the greatest players in the world ...

You think that, do you? Look, I'll tell you a story. Somebody – I can't any longer remember who – put my name forward for rugby's Hall of Fame. So, at the appointed hour, I found myself in London. To be specific, in the same de luxe hotel lift as Frik du Preez, Colin Meads and Gareth Edwards. My immediate impulse was to say: 'Excuse me, gentlemen, I must have got in the wrong lift ...' I had the feeling that I was somewhere where I shouldn't have been. It was a bizarre sensation.

'Our model of what a captain should be,' Philippe Saint-André and Philippe Dintrans have both said, 'is Jean-Pierre Rives.' Doesn't that at least carry some weight?

Again, I get the feeling that I have created a false impression. The truth is that the only reason I may have stood out is due to my teammates. They performed the essential role in helping me out.

But you enjoyed the role of creating a group and sensing it come together around yourself?

Nothing of the kind. I never did a thing ... I always said that in a France XV there are fifteen captains. It is not the captain who makes the team. The team makes the captain. If it was necessary then I assumed the task. When the referee came up to me to ask whether or not we were going to take a penalty kick, I had to give a response. But in actual fact, I didn't decide a thing. It was the kicker who, depending on the distance and the angle, would shout, 'I'm coming,' or, 'I'm not going to take it' ... My one speciality was that, if the need to say a few words in English arose, I was unanimously proposed ...

Speaking of which, your performances were always a great success ...

The more rubbish I spoke the better it seemed to go ... That was my sole contribution.

You cannot disguise the fact that in 1979, playing the All Blacks in Auckland at Eden Park, your presence and pep talk galvanised the French team ...

No doubt because I was able to put into a few words the general mood of the team that day. But I can assure you that any of the others could have said or done what I am credited with.

So, to avoid any misunderstanding, the reality isn't what the legend would suggest ...

But it's probably best to stick with the legend. In reality, I am not sure how much fun an evening in the company of Marilyn Monroe would have been ...

What was your relation with the public, both inside and outside the ground?

My pal Bibi [the nickname of Thierry Heuillet, an old friend of Rives from Toulouse and fellow restaurateur] and I write the odd letter to Tony Blair, ever since the day he declared to me that he had my autograph. Without wishing to put him out, I had no memory of signing it for him ... I only mention that as an example of how I never had the feeling of having formed a strong bond with the public. Not because of a deliberate, conscious decision. For me there had always been a kind of dividing line, in my head, between what I did on the pitch and everything beyond it. I never took much account of the public. I never stopped to consider its perception of the game. On the field, the public is far off, even if, at the same time, it is there and it is thanks to it that you rise up off the ground and press forward. But it is far away.

Do you mean that the crowd is so apart that it does not really understand what is going on on the pitch?

It's not so much that it doesn't follow what is happening, more that its viewpoint is different. What the crowd sees is not the same, because it is watching the players, while the players are watching the ball. The ball meanwhile isn't watching anybody and bounces wherever it wants to. It's an interesting situation. And, nowadays, you also have stewards watching the crowd, not the match. Finally, don't forget that different spectators see different aspects of what is going on. It's intriguing and quite amusing but all that concerns just one event.

What did you see when you were on the pitch?

Not a lot. It's the smells I remember more.

Such as cut grass?

No, I was never crazy about that particular smell. Because I don't think spring and summer are the seasons to be playing rugby. Rugby is winter.

And winter is mud, rain and cold ...?

That's true enough, but then rugby is a sport, not a game.

What smells have stayed with you?

Those of different grounds; above all their surrounding towns. In Britain it was like coal or peat burning. When you get to the stadium you find that you are in the middle of a residential area. You can smell the steam coming out of the hot dog stands. The first time you don't associate this atmosphere with anything. Then the second, like one of Pavlov's dogs, you know a match is about to take place and, automatically, you start to prepare yourself. Next, you are down in the changing room, with its particular smell: half disinfectant, half camphor. Even today that smell can take me back to when I was a novice. There's a brand of toothpaste that I can get when I'm in Ireland or which my friend Brian Loughney buys for me, which almost brings that back. It evokes rugby. Rather turpy.

The pre-match smell?

When you sniff that, you know you are about to get going ...

Can you talk about memories linked to touch?

I liked the feel of the changing room door handle. That told me that the game was over and we could now get changed (*laughs*) ...

To catch the ball and have it in your hands must be quite a sensation, though?

Not for me because, oddly, I am not a tactile kind of person.

Don't you think that grabbing a jersey, scrumming down and tackling your opponent are also about touch?

No (*categorically*).

Holding the ball itself is not?

No (*irritated*).

Rugby is a touch game, though.

I am not so sure about that ... The ball is not absolutely necessary. At least, the way that I played the game, it was not really essential. For me this was effectively a battle, fought not with one's hands but with others.

Can't hands help to unite men?

No, it's head and body together. The real players are not hand led. They go in head first! They commit themselves completely. More than is actually seen.

So you consider the contact is made via the skin?

Just like the difference between sex and love, there is no comparison between the part played by a hand and by the skin.

Is it simply a question of modesty to speak of skin rather than of hands?

No, I don't believe it is. The man using his hands – what else is he giving? Is he showing guts? Is he showing balls? When you think about it, to talk about hands alone is to talk about distance.

Let's move onto the auditory sense. What sounds do you remember? Verdi in the Lansdowne Road changing rooms? The noise made by aluminium studs scraping across concrete steps?

No – more like bells ringing in my head as I found myself dumped on the ground, without much idea of where I was ... Boing! Like being inside Notre-Dame's belfry.

That happened on more than one occasion?

You could say. Apart from the bells I didn't hear a great deal, as I was half deaf. I wasn't there in order to listen. Which is why I heard nothing.

Nothing and everything was what I could make out, in an ongoing commotion that had a kind of symphonic effect. Impossible to make out a leading instrument amidst the orchestra's din. Even when the passage of play – or melody – belonged, like a vignette, to a soloist, there was always the hum of the orchestra that created a dramatic, otherworldly atmosphere. One in which everything got exaggerated. When you are there on the pitch, in real time, it is as if everything is, nevertheless, slowed down. It's something elusive. And so one enters the realm of ...

Of literature ...

Literature, sure, and personal anecdotes that try to grasp what it is really about and not something else. There's a hair's breadth of difference. Picasso had something to say about it, I think? There's hardly anything between fathoming the thing or not quite. But it's that elusive nuance which makes all the difference.

To return to the metaphor, how would you describe the engine noise produced by a pack of forwards?

It's a purring noise, everything in time. A very compact noise. With moments of acceleration, as the revolutions hit a higher tempo. All the tappets and sprockets are running smoothly, almost of their own accord, it seems. Everything fitting together nicely; the Yin and the Yang snugly interlocked. When, on the other hand, it is not running so sweetly, you become aware that there is nothing really that you can do about it. The engine overheats; the needle nudges into the red on the dial. Things are not the way they should be, without you knowing the reason why. I've had similar experiences as a sculptor. You have a conception; you put it together: it works. The following day you move onto another design and the whole day nothing is the way it should be. The joins are bad, the lines and the shapes too. And, again, you can't put your finger on the problem. On the other hand, it's the uncertainty which makes things interesting. Luckily, nothing works automatically.

Does rugby have a taste which it leaves in your mouth?

It's an unusual kind of sensation, almost the same that I have when waking up: not asleep any more but not awake yet either. That particular moment which never fails to produce the same pleasurable effect ...

When you run onto the pitch to play an international is your throat dry?

No. (*Silence. He is thinking*) What I do remember is synthol ... Down in the changing room we would take a sniff of it. That stuff could really get into you. I still have the taste in my mouth.

You received quite a few knocks on the pitch. Didn't that leave a taste of blood in your mouth? Would you like to talk about it?

No, blood is something different. (*Raising his voice*) Nothing to do with rugby.

It is by sight and smell that you perceive the sport?

That's it! You are looking, anticipating others' movements the whole time. That could be why I prefer watching matches on TV rather than from the stands. You get the overall view. But, of the five senses, it was smell that registered the biggest impact for me. I can recognise a ground by the smell it gives off. There were some I did not like at all; others gave me a good feeling.

Which did you not like at all? The concrete ones?

Actually, I have got no problem with concrete. What I don't appreciate is when a stadium is too open. Cardiff was another ground I didn't like. We didn't tend to win there a lot ... No, I'm joking: it's a great ground! But it's true: I was never that fond of stadiums where we lost. More than any other, The Arms Park made me feel insignificant. It is a giant carcass, a monster that emerged from the deep and came up into the city and remained there. A monster which gorges on song, emotion and tears, and stays alive for a long time after the match; when everyone has left, it is still alive. You only ever pass through stadiums. You do not settle down in them. That is why I have always regarded them as places where you can feel free. Places that are inhabited too ... by ghosts. Twickenham comes to mind. That is an extraordinary place.

Because of its tall grass, cut at ankle height?

No, because that is where I am conscious of rugby's tradition. It has an incredible aura of solemnity. You could argue that rugby today has begun its process of globalisation and that we all play in the same style. The English now play with more verve and we, the French, have become more organised. Everyone has always wanted to defeat the English. No doubt because they invented the sport. I mean: to defeat England at Twickenham with a try in the final minute! Not just to win but to thumb your nose at them. The English are not unlike their cars: they never break down, but they do occasionally come up with a dud model. And it's not so much that, from time to time, we beat them as that they do not win. You can win on points but they still have their style of play, which rises above defeat.

Besides France, is there another country you would have enjoyed playing for?

If I had not been born French, I would have been happy to represent Ireland. I like their sense of the tragic, their empathy, their taste for all things larger than life. In fact, I have a real weakness for them. Their dramatic fighting spirit. More than fondness, I feel a certain kind of admiration – in fact an admiration that is certain. If I hadn't been born French, I would have been very happy to be Irish. Or perhaps American, but not for the rugby – for Marilyn ...

4

Clusters of gold-tinged sparks shoot off the metal strips, immense twisted ingots. With the help of Walter, an Argentinian craftsman, Jean-Pierre Rives welds together these intertwined, rust-coloured lengths. His mop of blond hair falls beneath the black mask he wears. He crouches; leans into the work; applies pressure. He puts the helmet to one side and pulls out more lengths which he manhandles and pushes into place in order to assemble another component, complex and stripped down at the same time. These forms resemble giant ideograms, that have been given a third dimension.

The workshop seems to shake and rattle with objects colliding and at each drop of a rail onto the concrete floor. Hanging by a wire from the ceiling, slowly the piece rotates. Jean-Pierre follows this movement, prowling around it, then stepping back. He turns away, only to return and consider the meaning of what he has made again. Walter, standing close to the suspended work, has not moved. He patiently awaits Jean-Pierre's choice, ready to weld again. There are few words spoken between them. The two men, with precise indications to one another, appear to proceed along an invisible wire in the magnetic field of the steel sculpture. Nothing can distract them. They are at work.

A Bach CD plays, followed by the contemporary composer, Pierre Charvet. But the music gets lost amidst the crackle of welding. Later, placed on a steel footing, the generously proportioned work achieves an equilibrium. It is almost ten metres high. It is static but, at the same time, very much alive. It turns, without moving, as we look, as if demonstrating its dimensions and twisting, ascending form. It questions, teases and ultimately seduces.

Reclining in a green leather armchair, an exhausted Jean-Pierre takes an oblique look at it. Defiantly or in complicity with the piece? Only he knows. His forehead is beaded with sweat.

~

When did you first become genuinely interested in art?

Once I'd lifted my head up. That was the day when I started not just to see but to look. I had always been interested in shapes and colours. Once you try grasping their relationship and, with humility, place yourself in the centre of nature, that is when you set the mental wheels in motion. For me it's an interesting thing to do.

Previously, had you made any designs?

Everybody has their little designs that they draw on a notepad when they're talking on the phone, to while away the time. All I am currently doing is those telephone designs on a much larger scale. Strangely enough, the doodles I made then were not so different to the sculptures I'm constructing now. It is still a matter of inventing forms. You have just seen the process: there is no mystery to it. One scratches one's head, working out whether the best thing is to shave ten centimetres off or to add another twenty. One never finds the exact answer, because there is no specific question. But, all the same, it's worth making the effort.

You changed to painting for a period before returning to sculpture. And you have also framed your sculptures. Do these represent different universes to you?

No, they're much the same, except that sculpture is in three dimensions. Painting on the other hand involves theft. You take a perspective to give the picture a third dimension which it does not in fact possess. It's possible to use a little sleight of hand. Sculpture's harder. It can't be thought through; it has to be felt. One walks around a sculpture, because it can also be touched. I give mine a talking-to; rough handle and warn them. Occasionally they receive a kick – and we can have our stand-offs ...

The steel beams that they are made of individually weigh several hundred kilos. You need to move these lengths into position before welding them. Is that fun, heaving this steel?

I could do without the effort ... I think maybe the next job I have should be as a ticket inspector on the metro. Having said that, I'm interested right now in making even higher pieces. Too high perhaps ... Although I might want to construct on a bigger, more expansive scale, it's the machinery one uses which sets the limits.

You feel the need to keep going higher?

No. It's just a question of filling up space. The bigger it is, the more there is to fill. The same happens in nature. Take a tree: it pushes out into space. Art does – or at least tries to do – the same.

The vertical plane seems to hold a certain fascination for you.

I believe we are all drawn upwards. On the other hand, as a friend of mine recently said to me, since men first noted that there is nothing up there they have been drawn more to the horizontal. I am in between, experimenting with both. I sculpt horizontal forms. As for the sky, I don't know whether or not it is empty. But men can live horizontally, so to speak, even if the times are uncertain and no longer easy. Individually, each is essentially good. It is society that is the problem, the way it allows anything to go; men themselves are still able to resist. It's a shame: the dissonance between the two can make life difficult.

Before the act of joining it together takes place, do you visualise a sculpture?

Above all I am an intuitive artist. Sculpture is always the representation of an idea that has taken a particular form in one's mind. It's rational in its way. On the other hand, it has a tendency to reveal what is deep inside of you. Which, in my case, is not altogether neat and tidy. In my mind's eye I can see these forms both before and at the time that I am making the sculpture, but the end result never corresponds. What I tend to do is feel them from inside myself. I can sense when things are working. I don't look at what I am making. Which is a good thing, because doing and observing are not the same. One must not indulge in looking too much at what one is doing. You can easily fall into mannerism; you become self-regarding and that is always a bad habit. Occasionally what happens is that time passes – it may be a while or only a few days – and I take another look at a piece I am no longer occupied with and a hidden aspect of it will grab my interest.

Rugby & Art

That's when I say to myself: 'Christ! That's rather an odd thing you made there.'

You get a lot of visitors here at your atelier: José Touré [French national soccer team player], Denis Charvet [French national rugby player], Claude Bébéar [CEO of AXA insurance group], Thierry Rey [Olympic judo gold medallist] ... The door is always wide open.

That doesn't worry me at all. I carry on with my work, whatever it is that I am doing. I am reasonably easy going. Deep down, I am a loner who likes to have a bit of action going on around him. To be completely alone, surrounded by silence, is not something I like. The people who drop by are mostly friends, old mates. You know, I didn't expect to end up being an abstract artist; it can still astonish me. The shapes I make are not intended to signify anything beyond themselves. Look at them: nobody is about to imagine my sculptures represent a tree or a chicken or a racehorse or a country priest. But there does come a moment when a consensus begins to build around a sculpture. As if a form of acceptance is taking place. As if we are all potential sculptors, operating on the same wavelength. That's astonishing too. It happens every time. I often presume that a person will say they don't particularly like the sculpture or that they are surprised that I am asking for their opinion

85

about it. But it doesn't happen. Everyone gets involved, gives their opinion, has a go at moving this or that piece. At the end we often have the same kind of feeling about them. Sculptors move about in the dark. We try to find our way along a wire, without having a settled idea of where we are going. So, from time to time, it is good to be reassured by what others have to say.

But not everybody gives an opinion ... Presumably there are a fair number of sculptures that you work on by yourself without getting any feedback.

I do pretty well all of them myself (*smiles*). They are my pieces. It is me who gives them their meaning, even if someone latches onto it at the moment they see the sculpture coming to fruition.

Being an artist: is that also about becoming acquainted with other artists? For example, your friends Albert Féraud and Ladislas Kijno?

As a general rule if one takes up sailing one meets other sailors. And the further out to sea one goes, the more likely one is to be at large with the more adept seafarers. I am not saying that I have travelled particularly far. They, however, have been around the world. I just happened to bump into them ... The original meeting was fairly extraordinary and the story has continued. Each morning I go round to Albert's with some croissants. As for Kijno, I telephone him frequently and we see each other on a regular basis. Two encounters like that are bound to influence the path one's life takes ... I have a vivid memory of how I first came across Albert. It was at Maurice Arnald's in Clermont-Ferrand. That day I found myself brought to a standstill. I was glued to the spot, amazed and dumbfounded. In irons bound. I didn't yet know who Albert was. I carried on looking at the piece, drinking it in. I asked who the sculptor was, where it came from. That was how I discovered Albert Féraud.

Albert Féraud... Albert Ferrasse ...

Why not ... Nevertheless, I think that Albert Ferrasse has been drawn to a different kind of life ... (*resuming his train of thought*) Then, thanks to a good friend, who got in touch with Albert Féraud, I went and had lunch at his house. I went into his studio and have remained there, you might say, ever since. That became my world. Just like, if you enjoy reading, one book leads to the next, or mutual friends get introduced, a sculpture can lead you to a painting and a sculptor to a painter. Another painter can take you on to another sculptor. That's the way one's new world comes about.

Was there a crunching of gears for you between ceasing to be a rugby player and taking up sculpture?

No, nothing like that. For the simple reason that I never 'played' rugby. What can I say? I always practised sport but I never 'played' rugby ... Nowadays I do a little less sport. I created a universe for myself, at the same time as I was taking part in sport. I am still in that universe, but practise rather less sport. I am going to get more involved again, but I am not sure it will be rugby any more.

You never experienced the small death of the sportsman who has got used to being an idol but who now has to quit the stage?

I never felt myself dying and I am not dead. That's probably because I wasn't too conscious of my earlier status.

The aura of being an adulated rugby player never affected you?

No. And again for a simple reason: deep down I never thought I was such a player. Even today I just go along with the game when the subject comes up, but when I consider the kind of people who I played with, I can't help saying to myself: that's not possible – those fellows are too well built, strong and intelligent for someone like you ...

No question then of suffering from depression when your sporting career came to an end?

I was incredibly lucky to have experienced what I did and I was bound to feel empty afterwards. On the other hand, I still remember all the players I performed with. As for everything we once did together ... All the old stories – they don't have a great deal to do with my current way of life. They're no longer my affair. Besides, I am not sure that they're that interesting to others either.

When rugby came to an end, did you feel that a new Jean-Pierre Rives, the artist, was about to be born? That a part of you, which had lain hidden before, was forcing itself out into the light?

No ... I never looked that far into the future. I had started with something and I just wanted to carry on with it. This became almost an *idée fixe* and I wanted to see it through. And since one idea leads to another in sculpture and one is always improvising on the same theme, I tend to have a lot of pieces which, if left unfinished, would soon be cluttering up the atelier.

Do you feel freer now than in your rugby-playing days?

Things are certainly easier. I have more time to do what I want to do.

5

Lying between a race circuit, a flying school, Meudon Wood and the Seine, Jean-Pierre Rives' workshop is something of a Jonah's Whale, whose steel jaws close at night, but which during the day open to give entry to a den-like belly where anything and everything appear to have landed. Harrows and fence spikes, fantastic fish and sculpted trees. Quixote's shadow casts itself across a Buddha's jolly form. Jean-Pierre has kept his early works, pampered and shining, as if in an undated Köchel catalogue. They mix with those of a later period. Distended and bare. Matt but ethereal. The walls are bare too, other than for the colourful, curlicued and puzzling graffiti sprayed on by previous tenants. The windows are cracked from welding spark jets. Whatever the season they let in the air.

At the far end of the workshop, a domesticated corner has been improvised. Three rather tired-looking leather armchairs and an upturned crate, which serves as a coffee table. An unpretentious haven in which to casually plonk oneself.

This was a day when Denis Charvet and José Touré had come to visit. They listened silently to begin with, surprised to hear Jean-Pierre, who is normally so sensitive and discreet, talking about his feelings. It did not take the two friends long to enter into the spirit of the occasion. Within a few minutes the ex-footballer José Touré and Jean-Pierre Rives had begun their own conversation.

~

Determination is a word that holds a great deal of significance for you. One could even go so far as to say that it characterises you ...

(*Singing in the manner of Léo Ferré*) 'Determination is not what counts, Good Sir ... Love is what it takes to interest her ...' More seriously – yes, I do believe that passion and the will that goes with it are what motivate a person. The desire to do something, with a little bit of natural talent added in. It is not a tap you can turn on and off. Everybody wants to do something, but some are more persistent in their desire. And stronger too. That is what makes the difference between success and failure. Desire involves choosing a path you are going to follow. And not everyone takes that step. Since I am someone who likes to finish whatever I undertake, having that determination is very important to me.

Have you always done what you wanted to do?

No ... Not always. There've been times when I have felt at the mercy of events. But what I tried to do was to come to terms with, and even master, these circumstances the best I could. To go with the flow.

Even where rugby was concerned?

Yes. It was not as if I ever had a special gift for it. Rugby was not my vocation. I know plenty of brilliant guys gifted like that. But not me. The only thing that made it all possible, is that I was not doing it by myself. I was amongst men I respected and the tempo of the game suited my way of rushing around (*he taps his forehead*). My wilful type of game, if I can put it like that ...

What is it that makes rugby such a passionate sport, and one that particularly appealed to you?

It's a game for men ... Whether you enter it head or hands first or shoulder charge your way into it, everyone's welcome to come and play. Toothbrush travelling reps; washing machine salesmen. The nuts and bolts of the game, its technical side, was something I was always happy to leave to one side. The simple fact of playing was what interested me more.

In saying that, you are not bothered that you might be taken for ...

... Someone playing the part of a simpleton? I am past the age of caring! I realise that people might consider that I am being hypocritical too, but I have already mentioned that I never thought of myself as being a great player.

Rugby nevertheless has served some purpose if it has helped you move onto the dreamed-about life of an artist?

It's true that rugby has helped me, thanks to some unusual encounters, to be in this workshop today, leading the life I want to, bolting bits of steel together, in spite of not having had any kind of manual experience before. That shows that rugby can give men a prod in a direction they would not normally have thought of. That it allows them to go beyond the limitations which most people set themselves.

José Touré – But the man comes first. The sport may provide the opportunity for contact and getting to know one another but, if the individual himself lacks character, if he is not altruistic, then he will never be able to share certain emotions. In sport this depends on the man. It might not seem so on the big occasions, since everything is amplified and the focus is the 'great goal' or the 'great try'; nevertheless, it is the individual who makes these moments happen. Not the sport itself. I don't agree with the way that the media these days is preoccupied with sport as a subject and ignores the men involved.

J-P Rives – You could say that about rugby too, but since we are on the subject of football: does it make the man or does the man make his sport?

J Touré – You may be the most technically gifted player in the world but, yes, it's the man the fans go to see and who makes the difference. What he expresses from within himself is what counts. That's what draws us players to sport too: the possibility of expressing what is inside of us.

J-P Rives – Even though I am rather clumsy with my feet I am sure that if I had met Michel Hidalgo [French national soccer coach] at the right time, then I would have been a footballer. I met an incredible guy called Jacky Rougé and ended up playing rugby instead. If he had been a classical guitarist, perhaps that is what I would have become too. How you develop afterwards, the pleasure you take in the sport – that's a different story.

J Touré – Maybe you just had the luck to meet the person who recognised your talent; who showed you who you really were: that you were made for playing rugby and that was how your involvement with others would come about ...

J-P Rives – No – I came to rugby in the same way that a kid gets taken to a museum or an exhibition. I'm not like Denis, who was brought up with the sport; he was bound to end up playing it. That was a foregone conclusion with the family completely immersed in rugby. The uncle was a player, his grandma took care of the sandwiches ...

J Touré – My father was a footballer but he never pushed me into playing ...

J-P Rives – Fair enough. But you still had football in your genes. You can't tell me that you were going to dodge the game, any more than a top rider's boy is going to avoid going round the track at Auteuil one day.

J Touré – When I joined a club at twelve years old the reason was to keep in with my mates ... For me, football is all about one's friends. The team I played for belonged to a village of two hundred people. I may not have been a bad player, but the icing on the cake for me was being involved with my friends. I would never have taken up tennis or golf ...

J-P Rives – OK, but imprinted in your genes is a round ball. Look at Denis: there was the possibility he could reach various different levels in the game: to become an international – which was the case – or to end up playing for Cahors in the Second Division, maybe only for a few matches. One thing was certain: he was bound to be a rugby player. Rather than having to be educated in it, rugby was fundamental to him. Rugby was part of him. But with me it's a different story; my discovery of rugby was by chance. On the other hand, what prompted me to come back for more has a name: Jacky Rougé. There was also my cousin, Jean-Louis Sirven. All of a sudden, I felt as though I had been noticed for the first time. That something was expected of me. To be honest, I had no more idea of what the sport was about following the first match I played in than I had beforehand. In those days I didn't really understand rugby. What registered was that, whereas before I spent most of my time either asleep, or at least dreaming, I now found myself running and running, jumping and diving. I was awake for the first time. So when they handed me a jersey, I was more than happy to become their general dogsbody. Which was why they wanted me to come back (*laughs*).

And then when the final whistle blew you disappeared back into your shell?

It was always the same. I never changed. I needed someone to wake me up, or else I carried on sleeping. Ask my parents. I was certainly not a neurotic – more the tranquil type; subdued even. Not remotely flamboyant. No Ivanhoe!

How would you explain your transformation?

Easily – I am a natural competitor. Sport for the sake of sport does not interest me that much; the battle is what counts. I don't like being on the losing side. Only fools try laughing off a defeat.

J Touré – One moment you are asleep and the next rugby gets a hold of you! The following day you come back! There's something quite unusual about that. You must at least have some thoughts about the game and how come it suited you?

J-P Rives – When lads began to drop by to say 'Hi' and to offer encouragment and praise, I felt as though I was liked. I had come in contact with a group my own age who were keen for me to carry on playing with them. If they wanted me back then their friendship, I felt assured, must be sincere. It was not really a world I knew or understood but I had this feeling there might be a contribution I could make to it.

In the national side, who were the teammates on whose account you looked forward to playing again?

It was more about the group than any individuals. What I find appealing is the concept of a team. Added to those of play and battle. The group may remain nameless but it has its laws.

Did you find that some characters within the group are stronger than others and that they are the ones around whom it forms?

That tends to be the case. Also there are those who are good at excercising their influence. One has more in common with some teammates than others. It's only natural. Then there are some particularly fine vintages, when everything comes together. 1977 was exceptional. There was a time that led up to it, the season itself and an aftermath. Everything coincided to produce this story. I have known some great guys, like Pierrot Lacans. In 1981 we required a strong team spirit to achieve the Grand Slam, snatching victory when defeat looked more likely. But the group of 1977 had an extra dimension. Since then the legend has grown and there are always stories being added to it. Which did not necessarily take place. That help to reinforce the myth. That's the way myths work. Helen of Troy was no doubt beautiful but what, beyond that, can one say about her with any certainty?

Tell us about the 1977 Grand Slam ...

Before the games, there were already the fifteen of us – and not a man more. At the hub was Jacques Fouroux. During the tournament there were the same fifteen, something which would not occur in today's game, where all the substitutes come on the pitch. And since then the bond has remained as strong as ever.

J Touré – Was the 1977 side a new phenomenon? Did it foreshadow a different approach to the game?

J-P Rives – It foreshadowed nothing.

Denis Charvet – The only real innovator in rugby at that time was Béziers.

J-P Rives – What distinguished us was that none of the ordinary limits applied. We were a seamless group. Our victories helped to bring us together even more, although in certain matches it was that unity itself which allowed us to win ... It was a two-way process. No one could ever get the better of us.

J Touré – I wonder if someone like Michel Platini could have been the inspiration for the same kind of united spirit and then been able to profit from it, as though there was an extra player.

J-P Rives – No, I don't think so ... You pick eleven top players at random. Bring them together and you already have a very strong team. Something like Real, Juventus, Manchester ... Next, take fifteen world-class rugby players and organise a match against a national side playing for the shirt; you are going to get beaten ... Possibly quite heavily.

Why?

I'll tell you a little story. Moss Keane, who played in the Irish second row, a plain-spoken character, a force of nature, was thirty years old when he was invited to come and play a game for a Welsh side visiting Toulon. Travelling down he found himself beside a young player, barely twenty. The moment came when the young lad exclaimed to him: 'Moss, you are my hero. I have watched you on TV. This opportunity to play in the same side as you is absolutely incredible. I can't imagine anything better.' Moss, bear-like and not that interested by such praise, was scarcely listening. Later: it was time for kick-off in what promised to be a tough game against the French opposition down in Toulon. Now the essential thing about Moss Keane is that he plays a solid game. No question about it. Not afraid of anything nor anyone. A buffalo without the horns. The game got going and the first tackles were made. But Moss, always to be found at the coalface, was not that involved. You might say invisible. Scarcely a thing from him that afternoon. After the game, the youngster made his way over to Moss and said, 'You are still my hero, you know, but, when things got rough, there didn't seem to be much sign of you...' Moss, looking rather fierce, grunted, 'Listen, young fella, I really couldn't give a damn about it.' Later on that evening – a few beers later – the youngster returned to the charge. Obviously he couldn't grasp why his idol had been so elusive when the going got tough. He wanted to know why. At which point Moss drew himself up to give him an answer: 'For Ireland, I am prepared to die, but I am not even going to take a knock for a bunch of lousy Welshmen!' There you have the answer to your original question. You can have the best players in the world and put them up against a determined Portuguese side – I am talking about rugby, not football – but if they stand around with their hands in their pockets, they are going to run into difficulties ...

You mean talent will not achieve much without the desire to play for one another, without mutual esteem?

D Charvet – I went with the British Barbarians to Moscow and we lost against the Russians ... But, in spite of what Jean-Pierre says, it is possible to make a random selection of the best players and go and win important matches against national sides. Look at the British Lions. When they go on tour they get some incredible results against Australia, New Zealand, South Africa ...

J-P Rives – That's just what I am saying. They are on tour together, not playing a match in isolation. It's the before and after which make the difference.

6

Great excitement and effusiveness: a gathering of friends. Thierry Rey, José Touré and Denis Charvet, accompanied by their wives, partners and children, have come to spend some of the weekend together at the workshop. Plates of food are spread around the 'coffee table' and the workbench and on top of a pair of fridges. The kids slalom between the sculptures on roller skates. An irregular wigwam of bikes blocks the entrance. Everyone, it seems, is in a good mood on a day when the workshop resounds more to the sound of loud conversation than the construction of a new sculpture.

Overlapping snatches of talk in which points of view, laughter or a piece of good news are being exchanged. Every now and again, Jean-Pierre goes over to contemplate some elements awaiting welding – he hesitates in front of them, uncertain whether he has achieved the right arrangement. He readjusts a length, altering its movement towards a new joint, before sitting down once more. But the urge to pursue his train of thought has got a hold of him. Up he gets again. His shifting silhoutte in the chiaroscuro, created by light entering the atelier's expansive main opening, is all the encouragement required for one or two to go and join him, searching for the right piece amongst a jumble of old metal.

They return with their steel trophy secured on the hydraulic work platform. Attention now shifts further within the workshop. Those scraps of metal that a minute ago had lain discarded are now spread out, and in the crackling act of welding the glimmering piece starts to take its form. The entire company gathers around the complementary pair of the blond Jean-Pierre and his rusty work. It's not entirely finished, as the artist knows, but for now: enough. Time to let it breathe and to have a coffee.

~

You have said that rugby is like a dream world. When you were a player, did you feel distanced from the world, as though you were in a dream?

I think that goes for all sports. And the reason is the same. You are the little prodigy of your village, town or country. From the age of fifteen, maybe even earlier in the case of footballers, you are taken care of. Until you are thirty. Weekends are taken care of. The thought of taking your childhood sweetheart to the cinema does not occur to you. It's as if you wouldn't know how. You don't have the first idea how to go about buying an aeroplane ticket because someone else does it for you. You don't even know that you possess a suitcase because another person has been there to carry it. There's not basically a great deal you do know, since you have never done anything. Then, at thirty, you are told: 'That's all. Your time is up!' And you are thrown out onto the street. You turn in on yourself, but, subconsciously, you are hoping that someone will come and sort everything out for you. You don't go anywhere because you don't know how. You want to fly off somehwere, but you haven't been handed your ticket.

And you need to find a job ...

Which is the moment you discover that not only are all the people who were looking after you no longer there but that, also, the 9 to 5 life does not particularly suit you. In any case man is not here simply to work ... If he were he would have cottoned on by now. Personally I find graft exhausting. So, quite quickly, I became more aware than I had been at the time that there had always been someone around to help. The change in life was not something I was prepared for. It was a difficult period. Imagine the trauma as you have your game, or toy, taken away from you. The thing for which you lived, for which you were intended, trained and conditioned yourself for is now gone ... When I stopped playing, I was affected. This took the form of dreams. It was always the same dream I had. I still have it – not so long ago, in fact. The typical dream is the one in which you are running out onto the pitch at Twickenham or the Maracanã. But that wasn't my case. I never dreamt that I was playing. My dream is always the same. And every time it's terrible.

Do you mind telling it?

Someone says to me: 'You are playing.' Deep down I know that I can't, that those days are over. This guy, I think to myself, is having you on, because you have stopped playing now. On the other hand, I have to play, because that is what he's told me and that's the way I am. It is a very realistic dream. The pre-match preparations take place. When the moment comes for us to head to the stadium I am waylaid by a stranger who holds me by the arms. I lose sight of the other players. I know that I absolutely have to get to the stadium but I don't know where the others have got to. 'Impossible,' I say to myself: 'You've managed to get lost again!' The match is going to start at any moment, but I am lost! The moment arrives and, inevitably, I am late. I am always late! Contemplating the match that is under way is awful: I wake up. As I do so my feeling is, 'so that's how it was, I never really played rugby!'

It is true, you do have a reputation for turning up late ...

I have been late from the word go. That hasn't

changed. What's amusing about my dream is that arriving late is the most significant factor in it. Other than that, the part of these dreams which is most intriguing to me is that in-between state, going from dream to reality.

That's a bit paradoxical seeing that your inspiration, like you said, led you to wherever the battle or the fight was ...

Ah! battle: that woke me up!

Do you do battle with your sculptures too?

There's a contest that goes on to produce the forms I am aiming for. I pummel and contemplate them, simplify or add something to them. It's strange to think of all the time spent contemplating whether to take away or reinstate a mere ten centimetres.

You have achieved quite a lot with your hands – rugby, painting, sculpture. Why then do you think of yourself as lacking dexterity?

Because every time I try to straighten something out I end up with an even bigger muddle on my hands. Every time I try to produce work the way it should be, I manage to make some mistake. All that I manage to achieve are failures. It's not without its amusing side. If I can't make a straight join then I bend the lengths into place instead. I think I am incapable of producing genuinely good work. If I have a go at repairing an alarm clock or fitting a letter box, building a train set or a model boat, things soon go haywire. My one speciality is glorious failure.

Using recycled railway track and RSJs left to rust on building sites ...

I have them twisted the way I like and brought to the workshop ...

The shared memory of you playing for France was of a player committing himself to the fray to the ultimate degree. Getting stuck into a tangled web. Is that the type of engagement you like the most?

At the time I started playing in the Five Nations, when you went into a ruck you could head all the way in. These days you need to be careful not to be infringing two or three different rules. Players nowadays are not allowed to get stuck in.

What is the greatest honour for a rugby player? To represent his country?

If you are actively involved in football or rugby there can only be one ambition: to play for France. It isn't in order to preen oneself on being the best but to stand up, not for one's country exactly, but rather the ideal of playing for a team at the highest level.

Given the choice, there are some who would prefer to win the league with their club. Footballers are most avid when talking about what it's like playing in the Champions League. You don't think the understanding developed between club players, and a club's traditions, can provide a similar sense of pride or even surpass the emotion of playing for one's country?

Not for me. Playing for the French shirt is what matters most as far as I am concerned. The match and how one plays, whether or not one wins that day, is another story. A club jersey is not without meaning. The shirt of France nevertheless symbolises more. The French Barbarians' jersey represents a spirit too, not entirely of the same kind, but strong all the same. They are both shirts that speak of an attitude, a philosophy of life one can rally to.

There are some players who look on wearing the French shirt not just as a personal honour but one they accept on behalf of their club and teammates, thanks to whom they have received the opportunity. Is that how you felt?

No, I think I can say I have felt something greater. Not for my particular club but for the whole of French rugby, which perseveres anonymously in order that the game is played across the country. It is those people you represent pulling on the French shirt, far more than your friends back at the club. They might play for the national side themselves, whereas the people I am talking about never will.

What is your relationship with the jersey? Touch or sight? Do you smell it? Do you like looking at it before picking it up; breathing it in before putting it on?

Most of all I think about not letting it get ripped to shreds, so that I will be able to donate it afterwards (*laughs*).

Have you kept one as a memento?

Not even one any more. Not a single one. None. And I am very happy about that. They have found better homes. I'll tell you something: I was on tour with the French team twelve times and played more than fifty games. That doesn't include the other tour matches that weren't Tests, where one was still wearing the French shirt, which takes the total to one hundred. In fact I must have given away two hundred shirts. I am not just making that figure up. I used to also take one from the team's laundry bag to give away. I wasn't harming anybody and I'm sure the people with those shirts are very happy and haven't spotted the difference. And the fact that they are probably very happy is what matters, as far as I am concerned. Knowing myself, I would have lost those shirts anyway. Whereas they won't have. I couldn't give a damn about the team shirt as a souvenir. I have preserved the memory of my teammates inside my head. And they have kept their jerseys in their clothes cupboards.

Watching internationals these days do you feel little rapport with the contemporary game?

Nothing of the kind. In the place of today's players we would do as they do. On the surface the game has definitely changed from the one I knew – because of all the rule changes.

It's also a bit quicker ...

Faster, maybe ... Though don't worry – we could always try going at that speed.

What do you think of the game today?

There's a lot about it I like. What I would change are various rules. Without trying to turn the clock back that's what I would concentrate on. I would penalise non-release of the ball. The player with the ball is the one who, without question, is responsible for it. I am not bothered if he is being laid into a bit hard, or having his hair or shorts pulled. It is down to him to pass the ball before he gets thrown to the ground or to release it then, or to kick it upfield. And if he can't do any of those then he's committing a foul. The opponent's job is to nab him and his is to avoid getting nabbed. What ought to happen is that when he does not get rid of the ball then it gets handed to the other side. Today it is the opposite ... A misplaced pass gets punished instead. Soon, we will end up like American football, where the only permitted pass is the clear-cut, decisive one ...

You feel that the rule you are suggesting would make the game more free flowing?

I am not saying that I am necessarily right. But, in any case, it is what I would like to see change in the game: if a player takes the ball to ground it should then be handed to the other side. If the man with the ball was responsible for it then perhaps one would see more live ball coming out of rucks and mauls.

You never particularly liked referees. The fact that there are now three, plus the video referee, must irritate you.

Not at all. I think it's a natural and welcome progression. Injustice is a terrible thing and this kind of supervision helps to stamp out cheating, fouls and dirty play which went unnoticed before.

Doesn't it deprive the game of a human element and make it a less passionate affair than before?

Isn't rugby already irrational enough, with its

ball that bounces in every direction, without having to add human error to it? One fellow to retain control over thirty others with all these impenetrable rules is asking too much. The game has evolved; so has the way it is officiated.

One could quite quickly reproduce the failings of American football, with play frequently being interrupted.

At least someone has the opportunity of making some money when they misbehave, with time for extra advertisements on the TV (*smiles*). No, seriously, how often does that happen in rugby? Once or twice, not more ...

You argue that video playbacks will keep a check on unfair decisions. An essential part of rugby, however, is to rise above all that. As well as being a sport it is a discipline ...

That is the difference between the British and the French. They like to say, 'The French are not disciplined.' What it is though is not that we are undisciplined but that we will not automatically accept a referee's decision when we feel it is unjust. Whereas they believe that accepting a wrong decision is a mark of discipline.

They are right, because the referee's job is to control the game and his decisions cannot be contested ...

Alright. The question then is this: is one on the

pitch to play or to attend a class? The ideal way to officiate would be if the players were allowed to sort out any problems by themselves, only seeking the opinion of a supervisor to provide an occasional ruling, like in golf.

You don't accept injustice?

I always felt more sympathy for McEnroe than for the umpire. What do you want me to say – that even McEnroe could sometimes be wrong? And so? Does that change anything?

Are you a bad loser?

I would prefer to say that I like to win and hate injustice, rather than being thought of as a bad loser.

Does that hold true when it comes to Rives-ball?

Ah! that's different ... In Rives-ball I am World Champion! This game began in the cellar at my former house, instead of keeping bottles down there. It's played with a Jokari racket and soft ball. I had a one-off court, that included the ceiling, the strip lights and the door frame too. I am the inventor and rule maker of the game, one of a handful of players, not to mention president of its nonexistent federation. For all those reasons you only stand a chance of beating me if you have played some warm-up games already. Since I hardly ever let others play, I remain virtually unbeaten ...

Amongst those who have played against you most often, who has succeeded in defeating you? Denis Charvet, Yannick Noah, Henri Laconte?

No tennis player, in any case. They get left in my wake. Denis is the only one who, in the odd match, has beaten me. When I was tired.

All the others have succumbed?

Yup ... Being unbeatable is a full-time job.

7

Spontaneously, a semi-circle composes itself. Regular visitors to the workshop remain silent, since they are likely to be first astonished and then genuinely fascinated as they listen to Jean-Pierre express himself so freely about rugby and to hear the stories he tells, with verve, of some of his sporting adventures. Without betraying or maligning the past, he unburdens himself of various episodes that had once made him happy, angry or sad. The shoving around that took place in the schoolyard. Then his time as a newcomer in the French side, which involved the same battle to make his name heard and find his place; to establish respect as well as the right to be different. Even more striking was to gain an insight into how much he knows about former players and his gratitude to those who preceded him. There is both an intimate and a rhapsodic quality to his relationship with those he had never seen play but with whom in conversation he has established a contact. This intimate detour is a natural one, and made with emphasis. At such moments his charisma is palpable. To interrupt an unusual moment such as this would require nothing short of an earthquake.

~

Would you like to have taken part in a World Cup?

Certainly. I don't know a player from my time who would not want to have competed in it, given the opportunity. But even more I'd like to have won it. I am not sure I would have handled getting knocked out at the quarter-finals stage well. Looked at that way I am quite happy not to have played in it. I don't have to carry the burden of being a World Cup loser around with me (*laughs*).

How would you describe its influence since 1987?

It has allowed rugby to become a global sport. Without it you would still have the Five Nations in the north followed by tours to the southern hemisphere. And vice versa. Another effect has been that the competition has given a chance to emerging countries – from Africa especially, although not exclusively.

You were one of the galvanisers of the French 2007 bid. What was your role?

If France had finally proposed Ireland's, Scotland's and Wales' involvement for some of the matches' organisation, I think I would have been quite open to that. It would have been interesting to try. Seeing that we are all stronger together.

At the time your words were: 'I am willing to be answerable for a certain spirit ...'

From the moment that the International Rugby Board members voted for France, one could see they realised this edition of the cup was not going to be just about money. Even if later that aspect is to become a dominant factor, one will still need to keep people interested. I volunteered to go and get the kids of countries such as Senegal and Madagascar involved.

You describe yourself as guarantor ...

(*Decisively*) I am not a guarantor for anything. All I mean is that it is vital that the World Cup should be a cup for all the world. Not the France Cup, the Île-de-France Cup nor the England Cup. What needs to happen is for everyone to become interested and play a part.

That sounds Utopian ...

People can think what they will. Personally, I like the idea of Utopia.

What role will you be playing then?

Bringing those who don't usually go to the stadium.

Won't it be more than that, considering that you are co-president of the Bid Committee?

I am not the organiser, as far as I know. I can't see myself dealing with sponsors and discussing contracts. That is not my business. My involvement will be more concerned with ensuring the event is one which can be shared by everyone. Making sure that the old are not forgotten and that the youngsters get invited to the party. If I can help to bring people together, I will be delighted. If not, I will push off.

The World Cup is bringing you into the spotlight once more and back into closer contact with the game. Which teams do you follow or particularly like or give you reason for hope?

I am quite biased about this. I don't go to many matches.

Any names?

Le Stade Toulousain, Racing Club de France, Biarritz, Grenoble, on account of Serge Kampf and Pierre Trémouille and Jacques Delmas. Who else? I am trying to think. Basically I am most interested in those teams where I have friends. But I don't support any of them.

If it wasn't for friends like Serge Kampf [Chairman of Cap Gemini Ernst and Young, and rugby club benefactor] prodding you occasionally to go along to a match, would you bother at all?

No – or maybe to listen to the noise of the crowd. I am not sure I would go in and join them. Just listening to the sounds can be a good way of following a match ...

In 2002 at the Stade de France you didn't have a valid ticket for the game against England and no one would let you in. You weren't prompted to force your way in?

No ...

The ticket collector didn't recognise you?

No ...

Were you angry?

No. I had already had a similar experience of being caught on the wrong side of the turnstiles. That was when I was captain of France. At the time I had bust my knee. Actually it was more a question of a sprain. But, whichever, it was one of the few occasions when I did not play. France were facing the All Blacks at Toulouse. My home ground. Naturally someone at the Federation had allocated me a few tickets, but I had given them away. So – with my pretty face and bad faith – there I was on crutches, at the turnstiles. One of the collectors recognised me and we started to chat. I told him – what was obvious enough – that I was injured and that I'd forgotten my ticket. He said, 'It's not important. Come on through!' But the other collector there wouldn't let me in, and explained to his colleague why not. 'You wouldn't let my brother-in-law in so I am not going to allow him through.' Both of us became more and more worked up and I couldn't see what to do about the situation, at the same time that others were pushing to get in. Then an executive of the Pyrénées Committee arrived on the scene. Normally, the appearance of such an influential figure would have been enough to smooth things over. But not then, since this Cerberus had always had it in for me. Even when I was a nipper he had taken a dislike to me. And that hadn't changed.

You were, all the same, captain of the French side at that time. It seems fairly extraordinary that they did not let you in.

Not at all. The collector who was quite happy for me to go in turned to the executive and exclaimed, 'Look who's here!' He looked at me and I admitted that I did not have a ticket. He said, 'You are going to have a job getting in. It's a full house ...' You don't say ... So I was a bit stuck, on my crutches, at the entrance. Fortunately, at that moment I heard Claude Spanghero behind me: 'Hey Jean-Pierre,' he exclaimed, 'quit messing around. You're blocking the gangway ...' I told him I didn't have a ticket, so he handed one to me. And that's how I got in ...

Do you reckon that you were being persecuted?

Since I was born on 31 December, I was always the youngest playing in the Juniors; it is also, by the way, why I've never appeared my age. This was the same character who was occupied, when you played for the regional team, equipping you with your boots, shirt and tracksuit. Then, if you happened to be selected for the Juniors at national level, he would come round when everyone was having lunch to take measurements. When he got to me, he remarked, 'Oh – you – it's not worth the trouble,' and with that he moved onto the next player and carried on taking everyone else's measurements. Just for the record, I was the only one of that generation selected to play for France Juniors. But that was why I always played in boots that were too big for me ...

Did it stop there?

No, there was someone similar who worked at the Federation. With him it really was a question of the little people striking back. I'll tell you the story. In 1984 I stopped playing. The following year I went with Pierre Richard [the film actor] to watch France play at the Parc des Princes. 'I wouldn't mind going down into the dressing room after the match,' said my friend Pierre. Personally I wasn't so keen, having only recently left that world behind me. The prospect rather dampened my mood, but that was neither here nor there. After a match there are only fifty-odd people who have a reason for being in the dressing room, but it was not unusual to find three thousand ... only a slight exaggeration. The match ended and we went down towards the entry door. I even had the tact to ask, 'Can we go down to the dressing rooms?' 'Do you have a pass?' the official wanted to know. Obviously not ... I didn't insist and we went on our way.

You and he crossed paths again?

Yes; you might have thought he was following me. On one occasion I was invited to watch a match at the Stade de France in the VIP Box. I arrived at the special entry and recognised him straightaway. I didn't have a ticket since Serge Blanco, who invited me, thought it best if I gave him a call once I got there. This fellow asked me for my ticket. I did not even make the effort to ask him to go and find Serge Blanco. Instead, I made an about turn and went and found a seat in one of the far corners with some friends. Which was just as good. And then there was another time, not so long ago, when I had been sent all the papers and passes you could think of. I got to the stadium. There was my old friend once again. 'Listen,' I said to him, 'this time I have got my ticket, pass, everything. But you are such a git that I am not even going to bother going in.' And I left (*smiles*) ...

The antipathy certain people have for you is nothing new ...

I have known it since I was quite small. I used to get called 'Bleach Boy' or 'Gay Boy' ...

You have been on the receiving end of the two biggest insults in rugby: 'Star' and 'Homo' ...

Yup. It doesn't get any worse than that. But, if I am honest, there was something about me bound to irritate them. It wasn't just myself. Part of the problem was that the press was always very indulgent towards me. If I played well, they wrote that I had played very well. If I had in fact played very well then they described me as excellent. When, on the other hand, I put in an average performance, I was still good in their eyes. If I played badly, that was when they said average. That's bound to annoy people. And after a while they start to say amongst themselves, 'We don't really like that guy' ... Particularly

124

down in Perpignan and Béziers, where they go to the sports page before reading the news. Plus I was the white duck in the brood. Which is fairly uncommon.

Did you feel that you were being discriminated against?

One situation is to be black in a predominantly white society. Another – not so different – is being fair skinned when the majority is dark. But when mistreatment can't be considered racist, no one tries to hide it.

Even when you were a young boy?

Sure. From the moment I went to school. Kids can be cruel. To beat up a black youngster is not good and is racist. Beating up a little blond is no better.

You are not about to tell me that it was in the school playground that you developed your fighting spirit, your taste for throwing yourself into the action? That would be a bit too hackneyed ...

No, look: redheads and blonds are always having to fight! With a ginger you're going to have to knock him down ... because he's been used from a young age to being shoved about. Same with a blond. The whole time they give you the finger: Gay Boy, Bleach Boy. So you have to fight. Why do Blacks in the Bronx take up boxing? For the simple fun of it? No, because they've been treated like shit all their lives, as though they were rats. For me blonds and redheads are the same as blacks.

The world of rugby wasn't really so different then to the schoolyard?

At least it was one in which you could stake a claim to be different and gain some respect.

How did you succeed in staying so close to those who, initially, you had so little in common with?

Thanks to what you might call the intelligence of the heart. That's all. That was the most important thing to us and what united us, even if some players had fancier footwork than others, their own way of looking at things or different interests.

When you played against other members of the 1977 team in championship games did that affect you in any way?

Before, when we were up against one another, it could be quite rough. Bit by bit we got to know each other a little better. That doesn't mean that when we found ourselves on opposing sides, which happened quite frequently, we were less competitive ... Even if we were now friends, heavy clouts were still getting administered.

Still, we now felt as though something was different. There are some knocks that happen to be part of the sport. They're different from those that are really intended to hurt.

Do you remember the first time you played for France?

Yes, I remember it very well. It was at Twickenham. What I remember about it most was being taken under Claude Spanghero's wing and going off to discover London with him. When Toto Desclaux, our trainer, asked who wanted to go and have a little wander around the city, the afternoon before the match, Claude announced that he was going to do some shopping and took me along with him. It was the first time I had ever set foot in London. So we headed off to Trafalgar Square with all its pigeons and then on to Soho, to have a look. Back at the hotel we found ourselves arriving late for the team dinner and got bawled out.

'How come you have managed to be late?' Toto Desclaux wanted to know.

Claude's answer was, 'We couldn't get a taxi.'

'And what did you buy?'

'Nothing. Everything's too expensive here ...'

Following dinner, Claude said to me, 'Come on, let's go and play a bit of poker,' which was how we stayed up late that night. Poker being the Narbonnais' game. We were able to have a good laugh about it during the match. Claude kept on asking me the time. He thought that I coped pretty well all the same and was saying to the others, 'You know what, I think yesterday afternoon he had a bit of a workout ...' (*laughs*)

Your mentor, Jean Salut, gave you some famous advice before the game ...

That's right. What he said to me was, 'Listen, to have a good match, just remember one thing. The English have got a big player. He's called Ripley. You'll see that all their ball passes through him. As soon as you see him, jump on him and don't let go. If you can do that you will not have had a bad game. He's easy to recognise: he's got the number eight on his back ...' (*smiles*)

Rugby, one imagines, allowed you to travel? What did you discover?

The way I travelled was rather like a cargo of potatoes or tomatoes. Down in the hold. I had come to play, not to mess around or be a tourist. I told the tour manager that I wanted to play in all the matches. Since I was there to play, I might as well get the most out of it. The training, more than the games themselves, was the hard part ... I suppose that at the time I did not have the same curiosity that I have today. I wasn't looking at the changing scene around me that much. I was there for the rugby and it was hard to get involved in anything else.

Didn't you regret that afterwards?

There are certain places I have been back to. And that is when I saw what I had missed before. In Australia, South Africa, Argentina. In Toulon. Whenever I had to play in Toulon I never noticed the sea and the hills, that there was a port there ... All I knew before was that there was a hotel and a stadium. It is not necessary to travel far to lift one's head and see that above the roofline there are trees and that in the forest there are cabins ...

The history and traditions of rugby were aspects of the game you came to later on. What were your most memorable encounters, the ones which marked you the most?

I have always respected the past. The day they knocked the Ernest-Wallon stadium down, I went there to salvage a lamp from the clubhouse and a framed photo of the 1924 team: Jauréguy, François Borde, Struxiano and Lubin-Lebrère – who had lost an eye in the war, not to mention being shot in the arse. I think it is important to look after these objects. As a record. I have spent hours listening to Kléber Haedens [the French novelist and journalist] speak with amazing fluency about rugby. An amazing man. René-Victor Pilhes, who wrote *L'Imprécateur* and is a great friend of Kléber and of André Brouat [Stade Toulousain player and President], was also there. They told me stories going back to the 1920s. I particularly remember the teeth of the wind. They were explaining to me that the rhythm of the wind was like teeth biting and that you had to time the moment when it would get a hold of the ball. For me these reminiscences were extraordinary. I was glued.

When did you meet Jean Prat and Lucien Mias and the others?

Every time I went on tour, I would send postcards to the veterans. To Yves Bergougnan, whom I had never met. One day someone tapped me on the shoulder. He said, 'I am Yves Bergougnan.' Then he was off in a flash ... I would write to people I had never met and idolise men I had never seen play. I never saw Jean Prat play and yet for me he was ... (*he raises his eyes heavenwards*).

Were there any you found disappointing?

Not exactly ... I met certain players for whom I had a high regard but who when you met them were not so impressive. But, in spite of that, I still respected them for the players that they were.

To continue on the subject of legends. Tell us about the first occasions that you played against the All Blacks and the Springboks ...

I have a lot of respect for individuals but not so much for institutions. The All Blacks are not outstandingly special. They have their aura, but that's their thing. It's not mine. I recognise that wearing the shirt is an immense honour for them. Still, it's not going to make me stop in my stride. There is no difference between an international who puts on the French, the Irish or the All Blacks shirt. The feeling is the same. The jersey is not as important as the man wearing it.

8

Issy-les-Moulineaux in the middle of the Seine. His restaurant, 'L'Île', reminds one of an artist's studio. There are aboriginal paintings, large-scale tableaux of Kijno, sculptures and lanterns salavaged from railway tracks or the top of old telephone poles ... A blend of iron, wood and colour. Jean-Pierre Rives does not wish to eat. He just asks for some coffee and a bottle of water to go with our last interview. Sitting on the banquette, with its view into the main part of the restaurant, it is as if there is a zone formed around what he has to say, which no one wishes to disturb.

~

You often talk about the village where you grew up. Was that an important place in your life?

I was born in the family home at Saint-Simon [on the outskirts of Toulouse]. The sporting side in our family was represented by my grandfather. He was a cyclist. Various bikes of his hung from the ceiling. I remember the shelter where all the wood was stacked for the winter. We had a big living room with an even bigger fireplace. The killing of our pig was always a jolly occasion.

Afterwards we prepared our own *charcuterie*. There was also a vine and a vat, that my grandfather used to make his own wine, which he then stored in barrels. There was a carpentry workshop too. Some dogs. The chicken coop, goat and horse.

Was Saint-Simon where you spent all your childhood?

No. My father was a soldier and we followed him out to Morocco. By the time we got back to France, I had a cousin, Jean-Louis Sirven, who was playing rugby. It was thanks to him and Jacky Rougé that I became interested in the sport. Not forgetting Mr Cassagné, my gym teacher in high school.

How did you come to the attention of this teacher?

One day he saw me playing in the schoolyard. I had got hold of the ball and in my determination to score a try ended up going through the gym window. No cuts, no injury, nothing – other than a lot of damaged property. The headmaster was thinking of expelling me but Mr Cassagné's reaction was to suggest that I join the local rugby club. He thought that I showed a special kind of energy ...

You have said that when your father first took you along to play rugby it was in the hope that it would wake you up. It seems a rather brutal way of going about things ...

No, I don't think his intention was at all brutal. He just wanted me to be a little more alert. A little less sleepy.

What sort of relationship did you have with him?

He's someone who is very intelligent, who likes to talk. Subtle; lively. There are a lot of subjects he is knowledgeable about. He enjoys repartee. Typical of the Midi: exuberant and excessive. Quite a sporty type. A bit of a character. Occasionally we were at odds. In being calmer than he was I was doing the usual thing of defining myself in opposition to him.

Has he ever told you that he is proud of you?

No. But I know that he is.

You would have liked it if he had?

(*Silence*) The first time I beat him at tennis I was still pretty young. I was already a better player than him (*smiles*). It wasn't hard to prove in those days ... But maybe we should have a re-match: he would probably beat me now!

Tennis played a big part in your life back then?

I spent all my time down at the club. My parents both played a lot. As soon as I was big enough to hold a racket they put one in my hand ... From that moment all I wanted to do was to play tennis. I can remember the rugby players passing by the tennis club on their way to training ... Tennis wasn't very well looked upon. I could tell they thought I was a bit of a sissy ...

What sort of game did you have? Did you patrol the baseline or were you always looking to rush into the net?

I was an attacking player! Who for every winner would make two unforced errors. So that was never going to work out ...

Your mother was not very keen for you to play rugby ...

She knew very little about it.

She did not know that you had become a rugby player?

My parents had gone to live in Abidjan for a period. A couple of articles appeared in the press because I was already playing at TOEC. On one occasion my mother came to watch me play. I was seventeen and in the university side. She had a good look but couldn't see any sign of me. Some other spectators said to her, 'Are you looking for your son? You need to go over to the other pitch. He's playing rugby. This is a football game ...'

Did she worry about you?

Following the *après-match*, when I returned in the evening, she would get up and say to me, 'Come and stand in the light where I can see you. Did you get hit? Where now?'

She must be happy since you have become a painter and sculptor, an artist. When you were a boy she had hopes of you becoming a pianist ...

I have no idea. I don't know what future she imagined for me. My mother was my mother who simply saw me as her son. She still does. She sends me rugs and jam and sweaters. I try to explain to her that I am fifty years old and that I am capable of taking care of myself now. For her, however, I'm still her boy. That's the way mothers are ...

Was playing for TOEC, Beaumont-de-Lomagne and Stade Toulousain a golden period for you?

It was the age of insouciance. Looking back, I have only a vague memory of the way I threw myself into the game. No doubt I learned instinctively, rather like when you start to ride a bike. I sometimes ask myself whether I still had stabilisers ... And the more time goes by the more I am amazed how I managed to do it. The same as the guy who makes a parachute jump and only later is struck by fear at what he did, who says to himself that he must have been crazy to have made the jump. It's only now that I feel any fear: rather as if I went up in a plane and got vertigo thirty years later. Curious ...

You decided to study medicine at university.

I chose medicine so that I could keep up with a pretty girl from the high school. She was very cute and, because our names followed one another alphabetically, I had always been conscious of her during roll call. We were both doing our 'A' levels. When I asked where she had applied to and if she had been accepted she said she was going for the medicine faculty. She then asked me what I was considering and, since I wanted to carry on seeing her, I said that I was aiming to study medicine myself. After that I never saw her again. Perhaps because I missed far more classes than I attended. To be honest, Dr Schweitzer was never my idol.

Your career path then headed off in the direction of the law, as a bailiff of the court ...

What happened was that I wanted to leave Stade Toulousain and go and play in England. The chairman, Henri Cazaux, didn't want me to go.

It was a fairly unusual thing to do at the time. The general rule was that players would stay at the same club for a long spell. So he sent me to his brother who was both very friendly and a bailiff of the court. He accepted me in his firm and I went to study law and qualified as a bailiff myself.

It is difficult to picture you as one.

It did not take me long to realise that it was not a profession I was cut out for. One day I had to pay a visit to a woman against whom a claim of money had been made. A big lady who had had a child with a taxi driver who moonlighted as a thief's chauffeur. She had been charged as an accomplice and I can't remember what else and had been ordered to repay a certain sum of money. I can still see the pair of them, her little girl sitting on the edge of the bed. They didn't have any money so it was me who ended up giving them a few notes. I tore up the court order and left.

What prompted your move from Stade Toulousain to Racing Club de France?

Lots of things. It wasn't something I did on the spur of the moment. I had thought it over. I didn't like the attitude of certain people at the club, the way in which one or two players had been moved on. The squad wasn't treated with much respect and I hadn't liked that either. I tried to find one good reason for staying. When they told me I would never play for France again that was actually the best reason I could think of for leaving. Those events nevertheless are not my main memory of Toulouse. It was just an episode. All I was doing was carrying on my way. To leave a club at that time was almost unheard of. When I got here nothing had been formalised or arranged. I had a little sports bag with me and that was it. I turned out for Racing's third side in the mud and, of course, I got sent off. I began to realise that I needed to sort something out, which is when I got together with Robert [Paparemborde, former international prop] and a few others, like Gégé [Gérald Martinez, former international scrum-half] and Claude Atcher. That's the way we got going: a minor miracle.

Do you remember the first place you found to live in Paris?

Sure I remember. The rue des Anglais, up on the seventh floor.

Was there already a 'Racing' ethos at that time?

'Showbiz' was getting going. We had our soundtrack playing in the dressing room. The backs sprayed their boots pink. So the easygoing atmosphere could not have been more different from what I had been used to in the south. Generally, I found rugby much more liberating in the north. When I mentioned going to train more regularly, Robert's words were, 'Look here, Jean-Pierre, you haven't been yet. If you start going now, that's going to piss me off big time.' So I didn't insist.

Robert Paparemborde was your great friend, your brother?

It's a funny thing. We didn't use to talk all that much, yet I think he probably communicated most with me. More than with his wife. There were times when she would come to see me when she wasn't sure what was going on. Sometimes I was better informed than her ... It was the same with Jean-Claude [Skrela, former international flanker]. Regardless of him being early to bed and me not. There was something indefinable between Robert and myself. Plenty of things that were allowed to remain unspoken ...

You miss him ...

I have some feeling for every guy I played with. With Robert, it's special. He is still here ... (*after a long silence*) There's Robert and the others who are here, and those who have now ... That's just part of the story. Look what that's made me do ... (*He wipes his eyes*) ... The story isn't over.

The barriers one erects to retain emotions or keep them at bay are not that secure ... I had a hard time when Robert passed away. He's still there inside me, with the others. Between us all, Jean-Claude [Skrela], la Palme [Michel Palmié], Jeff [Jean-François Imbernon] ... there's a lot of affection. Maybe we don't have a great deal to say to one another. The important thing for me is to maintain the spirit of what we achieved. And Robert was at the heart of that ...

Who lives in the house at Saint-Simon now?

My brother. Which is good.

Would you like to have stayed there yourself?

I am not one for nostalgia. It used to be a village. Now it has grown into a small town, with all the problems you get with a bigger population. Still, that is what is known as progress.

Could progress also cast its shadow over rugby?

Is rugby going to become 'Americanised' or 'Europeanised'? To change its character? And? Does that matter so much? It will become something or other, that is for certain. Whether one plays with one's head or feet or hands – is it that important? Why be concerned about wearing plastic shoulder pads or cotton earplugs? The important thing is not 'what' but 'why': why will one still play rugby? The attitude of future players is what counts. Beyond that, I am not particularly concerned whether plastic helmets or shoulder pads made out of – who knows – chewing gum are introduced, or whether one passes the ball over one's head or through one's legs. So long as the spirit of the game remains intact. Or even becomes better than it is now. So long as it can provide some meaning to life and help one to live better.

What would your response be to a kid who asked you: 'Tell me, Mister, what's the reason for playing rugby?'

Why play rugby? ... What if a child asked me that? (*he considers the question for a long while*) Maybe it's not so much the 'why' as the 'who'. And the 'who' has got to be others – from whom, if you know how, you will get a lot back. More than you give them.

APHORISMS

RUGBY

It is not by eating three leaves of lettuce washed down with a glass of water that one gets a rugby player. A sad rugby would emerge out of that diet. Going out onto a rugby pitch, in the knowledge that one is about to suffer, one needs to be happy to be alive. Without this lively spirit it will not be long before rugby dies.

Better to be offside than off-colour.

To play for the Barbarians was an event invested with great significance for me. It was as though before I had been passing by a church which that day I finally entered.

The Grand Slam is important but what really counts are the games themselves – the sum of which then add up. It is similar to a film, which is nothing more than a series of scenes joined together.

It is not through bad matches that great players come to light, though it is clear that great players have bad matches.

Southern hemisphere players are amazing but, at the risk of being taken seriously, I wonder if having even musclebound cheeks is such a good idea. How can you pass the ball if you are unable to smile?

Summer ends under the linden trees and autumn often starts as the grapes are being harvested. This is the moment when the new rugby season begins; a curious moment, where tea infusions and red wine coincide.

ENGLAND

Going back a long time the English have been smudging our metres with their inches and putting their feet in the culinary arts – especially at the hour of the post-match dinner.

The British don't eat, they fill themselves up. Instead of going abroad on a visit, they colonise. That's the way they are. And history shows that when there has been no country left for them to invade they have started colonising themselves.

Twickenham is a temple, regardless of whether the English have disguised it as a greenhouse.

I am not sure if heaven exists, but I am sure there are one or two intimations of it, such as Twickenham.

If you want to gain British interest in a war, call it sport. If you want the French to be interested in sport, call it a war.

IRELAND

The main difference between an Irishman and a Briton is that an Irishman is not British.

POLITICS

I belong to a party of one, which does not prevent intra-party strife from occasionally arising.

A lie is what you tell an individual. Politics is when you do not tell the truth to more than one person.

HIMSELF

I love friendship.

Friendship is a noble word, often applied to rugby players and their sport. Can the friendship between two men stand up to a cruise with their wives, offspring and dogs?

I live one day at a time and do not concern myself with the big philosophical questions. I would be very happy if people did not ask too many about myself.

When everything is in working order, I run like clockwork. But I do stop quite frequently ...
To be one has to do.

All the overwrought quarrels in the world are not worth one man's passion.

The essential thing is not to succeed but to have tried.

I have such a poor memory that I can't even recall if I once had one.

Having led the kind of life I have, I am not entitled to regrets. I am not nostalgic. Though nor am I concerned about tomorrow. Because when I start thinking about it, it is already today.

I do not pretend to please everyone. In fact, I think I have been more liked than I might have expected, or deserved, to be. I believe in neither fate nor chance, but I would not wish to go so far in the other direction as to say: merit has got me everything I have.

I enjoy travel. Once I get there.

I have never had the opportunity to miss a plane for a good reason. Nevertheless, I have missed quite a few. That is because I am sporting and like to give the plane a fair chance of getting away.

Originally I lived in the provinces. Then I came to Paris. 'I am going to the woods,' here does not have quite the same meaning as in Saint-Simon, the village I come from. Paris is like a golf course: the leaders are five hundred metres ahead; everyone else is five hundred metres behind.

Adopting Sartre: a man is made of all other men, and he is neither their superior nor inferior.

To enjoy good times does not make one good. One usually says this about others. If I was to build the House of Happiness I would make the waiting room bigger than any other.

After playing a bad match I would sign autographs with a small 'r'.

There are those players who, when they ended their careers, checked out by the main door. My exit was via the hospital.

MISCELLANEOUS

The human brain is composed of 85 per cent water. When you see what harm humidity can do inside a rugby boot, it is not so hard to imagine what gets produced within a head. That explains, without doubt, how things are falling apart.

SPORT

Having experienced a living death, I believe sportsmen are obliged to remake their life a second time. Which is not easy when you have been chaperoned every weekend for fifteen years.

I stopped playing when the ball kept getting smaller and the pitch bigger and bigger.

When we were elected to the Governing Body of French Rugby, Jo Maso said to me, 'I think I am going to propose the motion that we should do nothing.' I replied to him: 'I think I will propose that I should assist you.'

REFEREES

I have never understood British referees' decisions. They are incomprehensible even in English.

Three things that, as far as I am concerned, have no purpose at all: the pope's balls, a nun's breasts and talking to the referee at the post-match dinner.

I have refereed two matches in my life. The first was between two Catalan villages and I left the pitch at a canter. The second was between a French and an English team, both made up of advertisers. I blew the whistle every two minutes because it seemed to me the most objective and honest way of allowing everyone, myself included, to catch his breath.

THE TOURNAMENT

A tournament is Leonidas at Thermopylae; it is a kid laughing and men sometimes crying. A pretty girl in a lace dress, and the crossing keeper at Saint-Simon, who wears an extravagant white hat and talks about exotica to his parakeet ... A tournament is what a child dreams of and everything about it has the scent of camphor, of love and of what it means to be alive.